RADIANT RESILIENCE

Joanne C Pugh

I0079743

Copyright

---

1.   http://www.joannechristinepugh-author.com/

2.   https://www.collectionscanada.gc.ca/isbn-canada/app/
index.php?fuseaction=logbook.edit&publication=951056&lang=eng

3.   https://www.collectionscanada.gc.ca/isbn-canada/app/
index.php?fuseaction=logbook.edit&publication=951208&lang=eng

Table of Contents

Acknowledgements

Many people have shaped my life's journey, and for their contributions, I am truly grateful.

As a ten-year-old girl, I dreamt of becoming a successful author and speaker. Armed with a hairbrush microphone and boundless imagination, I'd write stories and poems, captivating imaginary audiences from the stage of my bed. I was blessed with angels whispering guidance, nurturing my aspirations.

However, the 1980s offered little validation for authorial dreams. While creative writing was encouraged, the pursuit of authorship as a career wasn't. "Find a secure job," they'd say.

Three individuals stand out as instrumental in bringing this book to life.

First, my deepest thanks to Tracy Sedore-Drinkwater. One fateful day, Tracy gifted me a ticket to meet the inspiring author Peggy McColl. That decision changed everything.

Peggy McColl, the bestselling author of "Savy Wisdom," "Your Destiny Switch," and "Be A Dog With A Bone," was the living embodiment of my childhood dreams. Here she was, a millionaire author/speaker, radiating the energy I had longed to become.

Peggy's day-long workshop empowered a room full of aspiring authors, myself included. She demystified the path to becoming an author, differentiating between writing a book, securing publication, and how to achieve bestseller status. More importantly, she revealed that authorship goes beyond writing; it's being an entrepreneur running a multifaceted business encompassing sales, marketing, and public speaking engagements.

Peggy mirrored the whispers of my childhood angels. Uplifting, encouraging, and a champion of diverse writing styles, she instilled a belief, solidified by her own success, that authorship was a viable career choice. Finally, I had a mentor to guide me on this exciting path.

My gratitude extends to Christopher Michael Duncan, author of "You're Not Broken: 5 Steps To Become Superconscious And Activate Your Magic." Chris, a successful coach and teacher, shed light on how our belief structures – emotions, behaviours, and egoic identity – shape our outcomes. He emphasized the power of self-alignment, creating a new identity structure and harnessing the superconscious mind to achieve our goals.

One of Chris's most valuable lessons resonated deeply: "You don't have to become something you're not to live your dreams." He equipped me with the tools to cultivate self-awareness about my egoic agendas and align my true choices and desires with my superconscious mind, creating the life I envisioned and birthing this book.

Finally, I express profound gratitude to the wonders of the creative universe and, most importantly, to you, the reader. By choosing this book, you've embarked on a journey to create a better world, filled with more love, peace, and magic in your interactions with everything around you.

Introduction

Unleash Your Inner Power: Own Your Time, Thrive in Life with Radiant Resilience

In case no one has told you today, you are a phenomenal woman. Within your being are the seeds of potential to become anything you choose to be and reach any level of greatness you desire to evolve to. That is your inherent birthright and no one can take that potential away from you.

What you hold in your hands is the guide to go within, and re-connect with your radiant, resilient being that has the answers and the map to guide the way for you to live your dreams, a life filled with energy, purpose, and the freedom to choose it all now.

The word de-pression means to "push down hard." When we push down our creativity and deny the expression of our true nature and purpose, we are not allowing the flow of energy from our heart to create with love and joy.

For me to write this book, I had to become my radiant resilience and reclaim parts of my voice and power again that had been lost in the misguided directions from society. I too, had to reclaim my true nature and purpose and rewrite the script of my life. Now, I want to empower you to do the same.

Radiant Resilience is your guide to reclaiming your time, energy, and inner strength. This book is more than just a collection of tips; it's a transformational journey that will empower you to:

Chapter 1: The Power of No lays the foundation, unveiling the science behind saying no and its crucial role in improving women's health and well-being. We'll explore the toll of unsaid no's, the impact of compassion fatigue, and debunk common myths that hold us back. You'll discover how saying no unlocks your potential for a thriving life.

Chapter 2: Unlock Your "No" Zone delves deeper, guiding you to identify your core values and set boundaries. We'll explore overcoming limiting beliefs like "imposter syndrome" and "not good enough," and rewrite your learning story to embrace continuous growth.

Chapter 3: Own Your Voice and Speak Your Truth, Ready to unleash your inner lioness? Buckle up for a crash course in assertive communication.

You'll learn to confidently express your needs, manage conflict gracefully, and develop the skills to say no effectively.

Chapters 4-10 dive into the practical application of saying no with **winning strategies** like:

- **The Art of the "Simple No" Strategy:** Master the power of a confident "no" with strong body language.

- **The Art of "Thank You, But No Thanks" Strategy:** Learn to decline gracefully while building bridges for future opportunities.

- **The Art of "This Doesn't Meet My Needs Right Now" Strategy:** Set healthy expectations and negotiate what you want with ease.

- **The Art of "I Need Time to Think" Strategy:** Gain control of your response for empowered decision-making.

- **The Art of "I Can't Commit to This as I Have Other Priorities at the Moment" Strategy:** Delegate effectively to create a thriving family and work environment.

- **The Art of "Now Is Not A Good Time" Strategy:** Prioritize self-care for a life of resilience and joy.

- **The Art of "I'm Not The Best Person To Help With This" Strategy:** Empower others by confidently saying no to tasks that don't align with your strengths.

Chapter 11: The Art Of The "No" Zone Defense equips you to handle resistance, guilt, and manipulation with confidence.

The Conclusion: You Are the Architect of Your Radiance ties everything together, empowering you to chart a course towards a radiantly resilient life.

Radiant Resilience is more than just a book to learn how to say no; it's a movement for women ready to reclaim their power and live on their own terms. Yes, it **can** be done! Are you ready to join the revolution?

Chapter 1: The Power of No: Why Saying No is Essential for Women's Health & Well-being

"I used to think the only way to succeed was to say yes to everything. I was wrong. Learning to say no has been the single most liberating thing I ever did." - Jessica Alba, Founder of The Honest Company

*****

Break Free from Overwhelm: The Life-Changing Power of Saying No

Have you ever felt like you're running on fumes? Like a car perpetually stuck in first gear, straining to keep up with the demands of life? This feeling of overwhelm isn't just a metaphor. It's the consequence of stress. Neuroscience research has discovered a direct link between what our brains think and how our body reacts/responds to our inner state of being that contributes to the outer environment around us.

Since this part of the brain plays a key role in your power and ability to say no it is the #1 key factor to remove the brakes, unlock the door to other options, and start moving from feeling stuck and stressed to reclaiming your inner power, your voice and your decisions to create and experience more love, joy, and satisfaction in life.

The ability to say no is a learned communication skill, not a personal defect. The good news is that you are not flawed or broken. Yes, you have a lot more choice over what happens on the inside than you know, and this chapter is going to start laying the foundation and show you how you can claim your inner hero with confidence and joy.

The Science of Saying No: The Hippocampus and Our People-Pleasing Autopilot

Prior scientific knowledge or a university degree is not required to grasp this concept.

The first part of our brain that we need to understand is the Hippocampus. This part of the brain is responsible for the information received through the five senses of sight, hearing, touch, taste, and smell. It processes the details from the outer world and forms memories and emotions. It works through patterns and relationships within our experiences and concludes our overall perception of "the way it is" in the world.

The hippocampus loop plays a role in integrating contextual details with the core memory. Your mind learns through repetition, and creates images that form pictures (like watching a movie). When this information gets repeated, it crosses through the neurons in your brain that create a path, looking for the same information in other neurons. When it finds the connection in another neuron, the memory loop forms. The memory loop helps us learn and retain information effectively and forms unconscious habits and behaviors we perform every day. It is constantly looping information through other parts of your brain and body, even while sleeping and stores information for future use to save time so you can get on with life. Thanks to this part of our brain, we don't have to re-learn how to feed ourselves, tie our shoes, or drive a car.

Our brains form habits and beliefs based on repeated experiences, especially during our early years. The Hippocampus plays a crucial role in this process. Its job is to solidify memories and emotions. For example, if you grew up in an environment where saying no to your elders wasn't allowed, your hippocampus would have stored that experience as a belief. As an adult, when you experience a similar situation, your brain stored that experience as a belief. As an adult, when you experience a similar situation, your brain triggers an automatic response based on that old pattern.

We can get stuck on autopilot, unconsciously following ingrained patterns that no longer serve us, and this is where the challenge lies.. Have you ever had a situation where you reacted to something and realized afterward that your response was unnecessary, and you asked, "why did I just do that?" That is your brain working on autopilot, responding to a memory stored from an experience.

The Amygdala: Gate Keeper of Survival

The Amygdala is the second part of the brain that needs to be understood as a contributor to our challenges when it comes to saying "no." This part of the brain controls the limbic system, and is responsible for evaluating threats and triggering the fight-or-flight response. It receives instructions from the Hippocampus as emotion, and the two are always in communication.

This part of the brain is unable to determine whether the information from the Hippocampus is a "perceived" danger or real and it just reacts. An example of this response would be walking along the grass and seeing a rope or stick that "looks like" a snake. If that person is afraid of snakes, they may yell, kick, and try to beat the snake (fight), they may scream and run away (Flight) to get away. Quite often, the senses of sight and hearing deceive us.

Another way the Fight or Flight system can respond to perceived danger is Fawn, which is abandoning your needs to serve others to avoid conflict, criticism, disapproval, or invalidation. Fawning is also called the "please and appease" response to fear.

The whole function of the Amygdala for survival! Its only purpose is to keep you safe and ensure your survival. It does not care about your quality of life, how much money you have, where you work, who your social circle of friends are, what music you like, or if you are happy as long as you are safe. This part of the Fight or Flight system is only concerned with the **quantity** of life, and the function is to keep the body alive.

The Shocking Toll of Unsaid No's

Did you know that stress, often fueled by an inability to say no, can have a devastating impact on women's health? During the fight-or-flight response, your body undergoes physiological changes to prepare you for immediate action in a perceived threat. It is a complex process orchestrated by the sympathetic nervous system and the release of hormones.

The Body's Response to Fight or Flight

- Increased Heart Rate and Blood Pressure:
- Heightened Senses
- Energy Boost
- Breathing Becomes Rapid
- Non-essential Functions Slow Down
- Muscle Tension
- The Return to Normal

Once the perceived threat has passed, the body returns to its normal state. The parasympathetic nervous system takes over, slowing the heart rate, breathing, and blood pressure. Hormone levels gradually return to baseline, your appetite returns, and other bodily functions resume regular activity.

This constant state of overwhelm can have a profound impact on our health. It is like a villain slowly chipping away at our superpowers, leaving us feeling drained, foggy-headed, and vulnerable.

Stress wreaks havoc on the body. It floods your body with cortisol, a stress hormone that can lead to:

- Weakened immune system
- Weight gain or loss
- Trouble sleeping
- Anxiety and depression
- Heart disease:
- Burnout

What is Compassion Fatigue?

Compassion fatigue is the emotional and psychological stress experienced by those who care for or exposed to the suffering of others. It's distinct from burnout, though they can overlap.

Why is Compassion Fatigue Relevant to Women?

In today's society, women are natural caregivers, taking on roles that involve supporting loved ones, friends, and colleagues through difficult times. This stress can make them more susceptible to compassion fatigue, especially in professions like nursing, social work, and P.S.W.'s who are caring for the elderly.

Imagine a nurse or personal support worker who pours her heart into caring for patients. She listens to their worries, offers physical and emotional support, celebrates their victories, witnesses their setbacks, and grieves their losses. This constant exposure to suffering, however, takes an emotional toll. Over time, she might experience a sense of emotional depletion, with all her love and compassion going out to others but nothing coming back to fill her – that's compassion fatigue.

The Impact of Compassion Fatigue:

● **Emotional Drain:** Witnessing the struggles of others can lead to feelings of helplessness, sadness, anger, and even hopelessness since these situations are outside our circle of control.

● **Reduced Empathy:** Ironically, in severe cases, compassion fatigue can lead to a decrease in empathy and emotional detachment – the very qualities needed for caregiving.

● **Burnout:** Compassion fatigue can contribute to burnout, a state of complete emotional, physical, and mental exhaustion. It happens when repeated high stress or crisis happens faster than our psyche or nervous system can process stress. There is only one way to manage this state, and that is by going in to a state of rest "doing nothing" so the nervous system can restore balance.

10 Myths Women Believe About Saying No

1. **Myth:** "Saying no is rude or inconsiderate"
2. **Myth:** "A good woman should always say yes and be accommodating and helpful."
3. **Myth:** "Only strong, assertive people can say no effectively."
4. **Myth:** "Saying no will hurt your relationships or career."
5. **Myth:** "It's better to say yes and resent it later than to say no and disappoint someone."
6. **Myth:** "Saying no means you're letting someone down."
7. **Myth:** "There's only one way to say no."
8. **Myth:** "You have to give an excuse or explanation when you say no."
9. **Myth:** "Saying no once means you can never change your mind."
10. **Myth:** "Saying no is selfish."

Thankfully, these myths are not true. In the following chapters we will provide strategies that challenge the validity of these myths and flip the negative beliefs to ones that empower you to say no and reclaim your health and well-being.

Beyond "Yes": Why Setting Boundaries is Essential for Caregivers

Overall, saying no is not a luxury it is a necessity. Women can prevent compassion fatigue by setting boundaries and saying no to additional commitments. By prioritizing their time and allowing for rest, exercise, and well-being, they can continue providing compassionate care without succumbing to emotional overload, ensuring they can continue to be the strong, supportive women they are. Think of it like setting a healthy boundary, a metaphorical "off switch" for the stress response.

Many women who are now caring for our elderly parents and our own young families at the same time also struggle with the concept of "compassion fatigue." We put everyone elses needs first, constantly pouring out from an empty cup. Just like a professional caregiver in a career who neglects their own health and can't effectively care for others, a woman providing family care who can't say no will ultimately have less to give everyone, including herself.

Saying No is Your Superpower To Move From Surviving To Thriving

Imagine this: You wake up energized, ready to tackle the day. Your to-do list isn't a mountain to climb, but an exciting adventure. You have the time and energy to invest in yourself, your passions, and the people you love.

Imagine the liberation of a single, powerful word. No justifications, no apologies, just a firm "no" that sets boundaries and protects your precious time. This little word, when used effectively, can become your secret sauce.

The good news is, you have a powerful weapon in your arsenal and although it might seem like a small word, it can be incredibly liberating. Saying "no" isn't selfish; it's an act of self-compassion. It's about setting boundaries and prioritizing your health and well-being. Just like a superhero can't save the world on an empty tank, you can't be your best self for others if you're constantly depleted.

Saying no to others is also saying "yes" to you and offers a surprising range of health benefits, both physical and mental. Dopamine, often referred to as the "feel-good" chemical, plays a multifaceted role in the brain. If the cortisol in the Fight or Flight response slows you down, then saying "yes" to you is how to release the dopamine and step on the gas to feel good again.

Unlock Dopamine, Unleash Your Potential For Improved Health and Well Being

Improved Learning and Memory:

- Enhanced Pleasure and Reward
- Mental Clarity:
- Reduced Anxiety & Depression

Improved Physical Health:

- Stronger Immune System
- Better Sleep
- Greater Energy Levels
- Movement and Coordination

Increased Well-being and Confidence:

- Improved Self-Esteem: The ability to set boundaries and prioritize your needs fosters self-respect. It tells you where your responsibility ends and someone else's begins. You'll feel proud to be in your skin and space, empowered to make choices and take action that align with your values.

Unpack Your "Yeses": A Powerful Journaling Exercise for Healthy Boundaries

Grab your journal (or your phone, tablet, heck, even a napkin!).You must write this down to get it out of your head and in front of your eyes. Your brain will perceive the information differently once you do this and it is a transformative exercise to see where you are placing your power, priorities, and authority over your life so you can take it back.

Reflect on the last time you said "yes" when every fiber of your being screamed "no"

- Where were you?

- Who were you with?

- What did they ask you to do?

- Who does that person remind you of? (Mother/Father/ Grandmother/Grandfather/Brother/Sister/Aunt/Uncle/Teacher/ Coach/Priest/Minister)

- What were you hoping to gain by sacrificing your time and energy? (Approval/validation/acceptance/belonging/significance/ worthiness/trust/love)

- What did you sacrifice when you said yes?

(date night with your partner, time with kids, night out at the movies with the girls, a hot bath and a good book, working out at the gym, going for a walk in nature, a nap, creative time painting/playing an instrument/writing/ knitting/doing pottery)

- How did it make you feel after?
- What did you think about yourself when you did this?
- What did you think about others?

Tapping the Vagus Nerve for Peace: A Gratitude Meditation for Stress Relief

The following meditation works with your Vegas nerve which is directly connected to your Fight or Flight system. By doing this quick and simple exercise throughout the day, you can regulate and calm your stress responses and start to experience more clarity as you move throughout your day.

Place your hands on your heart, Take 10 deep relaxing breaths in and as you exhale, express deep gratitude and thanks to that part of you that said "yes" for doing its job the best way it knew how to keep you safe.

Keep your hands on your heart, take 10 more deep breaths in, and this time as you exhale, express deep gratitude and thanks to that part of you that desires something different, to have the power to say no and create a different outcome.

Keeping your hands on your heart, take 10 more deep breaths in, and this time on the inhale repeat the following affirmations:

- "I now choose to live the life I love"
- "I now choose health and vitality"
- "I now choose to live my true nature and purpose"
- "I now choose to be the predominant creative force in my life"

Now that we have a clear understanding of how our mind and body work together to protect our survival, we can be more aware of our stressors when they show up and proactively respond before the situation becomes too serious. In Chapter 2 we will explore the life we are living now and how we can start to create the life we truly love with value, meaning, and purpose.

Chapter 2: Unlock Your "No" Zone: Uncover Your Values, Set Boundaries, And Own Your Time

"Don't be afraid to close your eyes for a while and shut out the world... It's okay to take a break and regroup." - Rihanna, Singer, Businesswoman

*****

The All-You-Can-Eat Buffet of Life: Why Saying No is the Secret Sauce

We all know the feeling: the constant tug-of-war on our time and energy. The pressure to be everything to everyone leaves us feeling stretched thin and resentful. But what if there was a way to reclaim your power and feel vibrant again? There is a way to confidently and graciously say no and create space for what truly matters.

This chapter is your roadmap to mastering the art of confidently saying no. Your starting point on the map is where you are now. Figuring out how to get where you want to go begins with knowing what truly matters to you and what you want to experience.

Here is the secret sauce: your core values.

These guiding stars define who you are and what you stand for. They are the compass that guides you toward a life of purpose and fulfillment. A core value is a fundamental belief that guides your most important decisions and actions. They are deeply held principles that define who you are and what matters most to you. Core values act like an internal compass, influencing your behavior and shaping your overall sense of purpose. These values form a framework for and guide your decisions that establish a boundary for what you will do and what you wont do, what you will accept from others and what you won't.

Identifying Your Core Values

Understanding your core values is a valuable process of self-discovery. Reflection exercises, journalling about what truly matters to you, and exploring situations where you felt most fulfilled can help you identify your core values.

4 Benefits to Having Core Values When Developing The Skill of Saying No

1. **Clarity and Direction:** Core values act as a compass, guiding your decisions and actions. When faced with a request, you can ask yourself if it aligns with your core values. If it does not align, it becomes much easier to say no with clarity and conviction.

Imagine Sarah, a lawyer with a full caseload and a devoted Mother. One of her core values is work-life balance. When a colleague asks her to take on a weekend case involving Sarah missing her daughter's school play, her core value provides a clear reason to say no.

2. Reduced Decision Fatigue: The constant barrage of choices can be draining. Core values help reduce decision fatigue by providing a pre-determined framework for evaluating requests. You do not have to weigh every pro and con from scratch.

For example, if integrity is a core value, you wouldn't hesitate to say no to a request that involves unethical behavior, even if it meant missing out on a promotion. Core values streamline decision-making, making it easier to say no without guilt or second-guessing.

3. Stronger Boundaries: Core values empower you to set stronger boundaries. You can confidently communicate your "nos" knowing they are rooted in upholding the structure of your core beliefs. This reduces the likelihood of manipulation or guilt trips.

Let's revisit Sarah. When she politely declines the weekend case, citing her commitment to work-life balance, her explanation is strong because it reflects a core value, making it less likely her colleague will pressure her to change her mind.

4. Resilience: Core values can be a source of strength when faced with challenges. They help you stay focused on your true North Star, stay committed to yourself, and navigate difficult situations.

For example: Trusting yourself and believing in your intuition, abilities, and judgment to make empowered decisions, knowing you can rely on others and feel safe physically and emotionally, and being trusted by others reinforces your sense of self-worth.

By aligning your no with your core values, you become more assertive and self-assured, ultimately leading to a more fulfilling life.

The Value Harvest: Journaling Prompts to Unearth Your Guiding Principles

Grab your journal, or your phone, tablet, or pen. The activities on the following pages will guide you on a journey of self-discovery. For each of the ten key life domains – from finances to family, career to self-care – we will explore activities that help you identify your core values.

Write down the current results that you have right now in each area of life below.

What are the actions/activities you do daily/weekly/monthly in each area of life?

How much time are you currently spending on each activity? (Include travel time or prep time as well)

What meaning or significance does this give you?

- **Income and Finances:** Determine financial goals and investment strategies.

- **Career:** Identify fulfilling career paths and work-life balance preferences.

- **Health and Exercise:** Cultivate habits that promote physical and mental well-being.

- **Family:** Nurture relationships and establish boundaries within familial dynamics.

- **Personal Growth and Development:** Commit to continual learning and skill enhancement.

- **Social and Recreation:** Cultivate meaningful connections and leisure activities.

- **Religion and Spirituality:** Explore spiritual practices and connections to the infinite.

- **Self-Care, Rest, and Relaxation:** Prioritize self-nurturing activities and downtime.

- **Volunteer, Charity, and Mentoring:** Engage in meaningful endeavors and give back to community service.

- **Hobbies and Special Interests:** Cultivate passions and creative outlets.

This time, imagine you are at the buffet of life and can choose anything your heart desires. What would you choose to experience in each of those areas?

- What lifestyle would you love to live for no other reason other than you love it?

- Do you want to sail around the world?

- Do you want to live off-grid in the country?

- Do you want to live the pirate festival lifestyle, traveling to different towns by boat wearing costumes?

- Do you want to live the laptop lifestyle, traveling the country in a bus or van?

- Do you want to live the millionaire lifestyle and live in a big mansion driving fast cars overlooking the beach?

On a separate page in your journal, go through the list again and write a **desired life** list with all the things you would just **love** to do/be/have for no other reason other than you love it. You won't be taking action on these yet, so don't worry about confronting others with your new choices. This part is about opening your mind to where you are now and what you want to create.

Being the authority in your life and decisions means being open to other possibilities and uncovering some awareness about what you like (or don't like) and where you may have unknowingly given some of your power, happiness, or creativity away to others.

Prioritize the top 5 activities that align with your values.

Create a Priority List: Write down your top 3 priorities for your life and keep them visible as a daily reminder. These are **non-negotiable** priorities from your list above.

Set limits on how much time and energy you can realistically give.

The reality is every woman has the same amount of time.

- 24 hours a day.
- 7 days/week =168 hours/week
- 30 days/month=720 hours/month

The only difference in the outcomes of life is how they choose to spend their time, where they go, and who they spend it with. Saying no with confidence isn't about shutting people out at all! It's about honouring your time and energy and creating a life you love with the people and experiences you truly want. It's about creating a life that radiates your brilliance, where every yes is a conscious, joyful choice aligned with your true essence.

Flip the Script: How Saying No Can Supercharge Your Life

Every human enters this world as an infant with limited knowledge and skills to maneuver around this earth. There are six statements we adopt in childhood that represent core beliefs that run on autopilot in the unconscious mind that limit our perceived potential and shape how we experience the world. These beliefs are not truths but learned patterns of thought that form your unconscious patterns and shape your behavior in adulthood.

These beliefs will pop up when you think about making changes in any area of life as resistance because the job of your unconscious is keeping you safe. Since you are still alive and reading this book, that's proof enough that your unconscious has done its job to protect your survival and quantity of life. It may not be running the best programming for what you want to experience for quality of life, but it is doing the job.

The good news? This **does not** mean you are a flawed or broken person. By recognizing this as a program running in the background of your mind and challenging the validity of the belief with new information, you can re-wire your brain, rewrite your life story, and build a more empowering unconscious mind that works **for** you instead of against you. It is possible to produce results with greater confidence and joy.

Any time you approach a new outcome from the "I am not...." perspective, you send instructions to your brain "I don't have the power or capacity so it's not safe." What does your unconscious say "Not safe, ok. Don't do that."

Let's break down each limiting belief and how it may influence your ability to say no and make changes to live your desired life. Look at your "desired life" list and choose one thing you want to do/be/have. As you go through the list below, consider which of these beliefs is holding you back.

Turning No Way into My Way: Conquering the I Don't Belong Belief and Taking Action

Scenario: Networking Event for a New Industry

1. Belief: I don't belong

- **Arrival:** You arrive at the event feeling anxious and out of place. You scan the room for familiar faces but see only established professionals confidently mingling.

- **Internal Dialogue:** "Everyone here seems accomplished and already knows each other. I have nothing to offer in this industry."

- **Actions:** You hesitate to approach anyone, fearing rejection. You might hover near the food or drinks table, avoiding eye contact and feeling increasingly isolated. If someone does strike up a conversation, you downplay your skills and experience. You might focus on asking generic questions instead of actively engaging in conversation.

- **Departure:** You leave the event early, feeling discouraged and further convinced that you don't belong in this new industry.

Missed Opportunities:

- **Making Connections:** By isolating yourself, you miss the chance to meet people who could become valuable mentors, collaborators, or future employers.

- **Learning About the Industry:** Engaging with professionals could have provided valuable insights about career paths, company cultures, and upcoming trends in the industry.

- **Building Confidence:** Putting yourself out there, even if it feels uncomfortable initially, can help build confidence and overcome the feeling of not belonging.

Alternative Approach:
Belief: I Do Belong

- **Arrival:** Take a deep breath and remind yourself of your passion for this new industry.

- **Internal Dialogue:** "I'm here to learn and network. Everyone starts somewhere!"

- **Actions:**

- **Focus on Body Language:** Maintain open and approachable body language (good posture, eye contact, and a smile).

- **Start Small:** Approach a small group conversation and introduce yourself. Find common ground by mentioning your interest in the industry.

- **Ask Questions:** Actively listen and show genuine interest in others. Ask thoughtful questions about their careers and experiences.

- **Share Your Story:** Briefly share your background and why you are interested in the industry. Focus on transferable skills and your eagerness to learn.

- **Exchange Information:** Collect business cards or connect on LinkedIn to maintain the connection after the event.

- **Departure:** Leave the event energized and with a handful of new connections. You might even have follow-up conversations planned, taking a step towards establishing yourself in the industry.

Beyond The Imposter: Conquering the "Not Good Enough" Belief to Land Your Dream Promotion

Scenario: You're Up for a Promotion at Work
2. Belief: I Am Not Good Enough

- **Internal Dialogue:** "There's no way I deserve this promotion. They must have made a mistake by even considering me. I bet [coworker's name] is way more qualified."

- **Actions:** You downplay your accomplishments during your performance review, focusing on your shortcomings instead. You avoid campaigning or advocating for yourself to your manager. When colleagues ask about the promotion, you brush it off or make self-deprecating jokes.

- **Outcome:** You don't get the promotion, further solidifying your belief that you're not good enough.

Belief: I Am Good Enough

- **Internal Dialogue:** "I've worked hard for this opportunity and have the skills and experience to excel in this role. I deserve consideration."

- **Actions:** You confidently present your accomplishments and contributions during your review, using data and metrics to showcase your impact. You proactively discuss your career goals with your manager and express your interest in the promotion. You engage with colleagues in similar positions for informational interviews to learn more about the role and responsibilities.

- **Outcome:** Regardless of the final decision, you feel empowered and confident in your abilities. You gain valuable insights and connections that will benefit your career, even if you don't get the promotion this time.

The Lovable You: Shedding Self-Doubt and Building Healthy Relationships

Scenario: Spending Time With Others And Long Term Romance
3. Belief: I Am Not Lovable

- **Dating Scenario:** You swipe left on potential matches on dating apps out of fear of rejection, even if they seem interesting. On dates, you downplay your accomplishments and interests, focusing on the other person attempting to appear agreeable. You might misinterpret playful teasing or harmless jokes as signs of disinterest, leading you to withdraw from the connection.

- **Friendships:** You hesitate to reach out to friends to make plans, fearing they won't be interested in spending time with you. You might become overly critical or jealous of your friends' successes, pushing them away unintentionally. When friends offer constructive criticism, you take it personally, interpreting it as a sign of disapproval and questioning your place in the friendship.

- **Romantic Relationships:** You might settle for unhealthy or unfulfilling relationships because you believe you don't deserve better. You constantly seek validation from your partner, becoming overly dependent and neglecting your needs. You might become suspicious of your partner's actions, misinterpreting social interactions as signs of infidelity.

Belief: I Am Lovable

- **Dating Scenario:** You bring a positive attitude to online dating, actively seeking connections with people who share your interests. You confidently express yourself on dates, highlighting your strengths and passions. You can laugh at yourself and navigate playful teasing without feeling insecure. You trust your intuition and end connections that don't feel right, knowing you deserve someone who appreciates you for who you are.

● **Friendships:** You take initiative when making plans and fostering friendships. You celebrate your friends' successes and offer support during challenging times. You are open to constructive criticism, seeing it as an opportunity for personal growth. You feel comfortable expressing your needs and setting boundaries in your friendships, knowing true friends will respect them.

● **Romantic Relationships:** You set healthy boundaries and prioritize your own needs within the relationship. You communicate openly and honestly with your partner, fostering trust and mutual respect. You feel secure in your relationship, knowing your partner loves you for who you are, flaws and all. You are confident enough to weather challenges together, knowing your love is strong.

"I Can Do This!": Rewrite Your Learning Story and Break Through the Capacity Barrier

Scenario: Learning a New Skill
4. Belief: I Don't Have the Capacity

- **Internal Dialogue:** "There's no way I can learn how to code. It seems too complicated, and I'm already swamped with work. I wouldn't be good at it anyway."

- **Actions:** You avoid signing up for that coding class you've been interested in. Even if a friend suggests learning together, you decline, citing your busy schedule (a real or perceived busyness fueled by the belief of lacking capacity). You might tell yourself you'll learn "someday" when you have more time, but that day never seems to come.

- **Outcome:** You miss out on the opportunity to develop a valuable skill that could benefit you professionally or personally. You might feel frustrated and stuck in your current routine.

Belief: I Am Capable

- **Internal Dialogue:** "Learning to code sounds challenging, but I am a quick learner. I can break it down into smaller steps and find resources to help me succeed. This could open up new career opportunities."

- **Actions:** You research online coding courses or boot camps and choose one that fits your schedule and learning style. You contact friends or colleagues who know how to code for advice or support. You commit to dedicating a specific amount of time each week to learning, even if it's just starting with the basics.

- **Outcome:** You gain a new skill and feel a sense of accomplishment. You might even discover a hidden passion for coding. This newfound capacity can lead to career advancement or open doors to new hobbies and interests.

The Imperfect Speaker's Guide to Success: How Humility Wins Over Audiences

Scenario: Public Speaking Engagement
5. Belief: I Am Perfect

- **Preparation:** This person spends minimal time preparing for the speech, believing their natural brilliance will carry them through. They might not research the audience or tailor the content to their needs.

- **Delivery:** They deliver the speech with a sense of arrogance, assuming the audience is eager to hear their flawless wisdom. Fearing any feedback as a challenge to their perceived perfection, they may withdraw from audience engagement or struggle to respond gracefully to questions.

- **Outcome:** The audience might feel alienated by the speaker's self-importance and lack of connection. They might leave feeling uninformed or even disrespected. The speaker, however, remains convinced of their perfection, attributing any negative feedback to the audience's inability to appreciate their brilliance.

Belief: I Am Not Perfect

- **Preparation:** This person might become paralyzed by fear of imperfection. They spend an excessive amount of time preparing, agonizing over every detail. They might be overly critical of their practice sessions, focusing on mistakes instead of their strengths.

- **Delivery:** They deliver the speech with nervousness and self-doubt, affecting the clarity of the presentation and confident delivery. They might apologize for perceived flaws or stumble over their words, reinforcing the negative self-image.

- **Outcome:** The audience might pick up on the speaker's anxiety and feel less engaged. While the speaker might gain valuable experience from the challenge, the negative self-talk could overshadow any positive aspects.

Balanced Perspective:

- **Preparation:** This person strikes a balance between confidence and preparation. They invest time in researching the audience and crafting a compelling message. They acknowledge potential areas for improvement and practice with a positive attitude.

- **Delivery:** They deliver the speech with a sense of authenticity and openness. They acknowledge their humanity and embrace the possibility of making mistakes. They connect with the audience through storytelling and interaction, fostering a sense of shared experience.

- **Outcome:** The audience will feel engaged and inspired by the speaker's vulnerability and genuine passion. The speaker learns and grows from the experience, celebrating their success and using any feedback as an opportunity for further improvement.

The Ripple Effect: Overcoming "I Am Not Significant" to Make a Positive Impact

Scenario: Neighbourhood Cleanup Project
  6. Belief: I Am Not Significant

- **Internal Dialogue:** "This cleanup project won't make a difference anyway. The park is always trashed. What's the point of me even going?"

- **Actions:** You skip the neighborhood cleanup project organized by your local community center. You might even discourage others from participating, highlighting the perceived futility of the effort.

- **Outcome:** You miss out on the opportunity to connect with your neighbors and make a positive impact on your local environment. You might feel further isolated and disconnected from your community.

Belief: I Am Significant

- **Internal Dialogue:** "The park is a mess, but every little bit helps! Plus, it'll be a good way to meet my neighbours and make the area look nicer."

- **Actions:** You actively participate in the cleanup project, encouraging others to join. You focus on collecting trash and debris, working alongside your neighbours, and enjoying the community.

- **Outcome:** You contribute to a cleaner and more enjoyable park for everyone in the neighbourhood. You might connect with neighbours you haven't met before and feel a sense of accomplishment and belonging. You realize that even small actions, when combined with others, can create a positive change.

Do Less, Live More: Finding Fulfillment Beyond the Hustle

Let's be honest: our society often equates self-worth with productivity. The busier we are, the more important we must be, right? But the truth is, your right to exist and experience joy isn't defined by your to-do list.

Saying no allows you to prioritize what **truly matters to you**. When you focus your time and energy on activities that align with your values and passions, you unlock a deeper sense of fulfillment. It's not about becoming a productivity hermit who meditates all day (although there's nothing wrong with that if it works for you!). It's about creating a life that feels balanced and nourishing.

Here's the shift: instead of focusing on doing less to prove your worth, focus on making space for the things that bring you joy and a sense of purpose. Maybe it's spending more time with loved ones, pursuing creative hobbies, or simply making time for relaxation. By honouring your needs and desires, you create a life that feels rich and fulfilling, not just busy.

Congratulations! Now you know what your dreams, passions, values, and life desires are. You know where you are spending too much time on experiences that don't fulfill you and flipped the script on some of the outdated beliefs that have been holding you back. You are clear, focused on your "why" and ready to begin negotiating life on your terms. You'll learn to communicate assertively, ensuring your needs are heard. We'll also cover how to gracefully ask for help and navigate negotiations to achieve the changes you want.

Chapter 3: Own Your Voice And Speak Your Truth: The Assertiveness Makeover

"The question isn't who will let me; it's who will stop me." - Ayn Rand, Author, Philosopher

*****

Unleashing the Inner Lioness: Lainie's Creative Awakening

Lainie, a brilliant graphic designer at a bustling advertising agency, had a secret superpower that was about to awaken. She had an inward silence, a wall she built around herself from the belief that her ideas were insignificant. In meetings, her creative genius simmered beneath the surface, overshadowed by the booming voices of her colleagues. When her ideas were blatantly stolen by coworkers, a flicker of resentment would ignite, then fizzle out as she mumbled a half-hearted reply, "Maybe that could work."

One day, a new project landed on Lainie's desk. It was for a campaign, promoting a revolutionary fitness app designed to empower women. As Lainie scrolled through the initial, generic concepts, a fire ignited within her. The project wasn't just any ad campaign; it spoke to the core values of her soul and vibrated within like a tuning fork that awakened the woman who yearned to be heard. When it came time to present her ideas, the familiar knot tightened in her throat.

Suddenly, she remembered the dog-eared copy of "Radiant Resilience" on her nightstand. She flipped through the pages, landing on the chapter, "Owning Your Voice." Lainie reread the passage about the lioness, a jolt of electricity coursing through her. This was not about being aggressive it was about owning her voice and speaking her truth.

Taking a deep breath, Lainie walked into the meeting room, head held high. Gone was the timid mumbler; in her place stood a woman radiating confidence. She presented her concept – a visually stunning design that captured the essence of female strength and empowerment. This time, the room fell silent, not awkwardness, but with a captivated hush. As Lainie finished, a slow clap echoed in the room, followed by a wave of enthusiastic approval. Her colleagues were astonished by the power and originality of her ideas.

From that day on, Lainie's Superpower was her voice that became her strongest asset. She learned to express her opinions clearly and confidently, her silence replaced by the roar of a creative force. And it all started with the transforming power of assertive communication.

*****

Are You Ready to Unleash Your Inner Lioness?

Answer each question honestly by choosing the answer that best reflects your typical behavior. There are no right or wrong answers since this is to gauge your current assertiveness level so you know what areas need improvement. It is possible to feel comfortable being assertive in some situations but not in others.

1. During a brainstorming session, you have a great idea but hesitate to share it because you worry someone might think the idea is silly.

- (a) Almost always.
- (b) Sometimes.
- (c) Rarely.

1. A colleague takes credit for your work, your response:

- (a) Stay silent and feel resentful.

- (b) Might mention it to them privately, but avoid bringing it up in a group setting.

- (c) Calmly and clearly explain the situation to your supervisor.

1. You are swamped with work, and your boss asks you to take on another project, and you respond by:

- (a) Agree immediately, even if it means working late.

- (b) Hesitate to say no, but might mention you are already busy.

- (c) Explain your workload and politely ask if the deadline can be adjusted or the task delegated.

1. You disagree with a friend's opinion during a conversation, you respond by:

- (a) Avoid voicing your disagreement and nod along.

- (b) Might express your opinion hesitantly, worried about hurting their feelings.

- (c) Confidently share your perspective while acknowledging their point of view.

1. A salesperson is pressuring you to make a purchase you're uncertain about, your response:

- (a) Feeling obligated to buy something, even if you don't need it.

- (b) Might politely decline but feel slightly pressured to continue the conversation.

- (c) Thank them for their time but firmly say no, explaining that you are not interested in the offer.

Scoring:

- Mostly (a) answers: You may benefit from developing your assertiveness skills.

- Mostly (b) answers: You show some assertiveness, but there are situations where you could be more confident in expressing yourself.

- Mostly (c) answers: You demonstrate strong, assertive communication skills!

Remember: This is a brief quiz and doesn't capture the full picture of your level of assertiveness. The following sections of the chapter will provide valuable tools and techniques to help you further develop your assertiveness.

Debunking the Assertiveness Myth: You're a Lioness, Not a Rabid Raccoon

Have you ever been told that being assertive is just a sugar-coated way of being a bully or bossy? That is a common misconception and a myth holding you back from developing a vital skill and unlocking the magic of assertive communication. Here is the truth: Assertiveness is the confident lioness, protecting her cubs with strength and unwavering resolve, but with grace. Aggression, in contrast, is the cornered raccoon, hissing, swiping, and leaving a trail of chaos in its wake. There is a big difference, right?

So, how do we ditch the meek persona and embrace our inner lioness? It's all about a few key practices:

1. **Know your worth-** When you know your value and express your needs, wants, and opinions clearly and directly, this becomes an act of self-respect, not a selfish demand, while also respecting the rights of others.
2. **Master clear communication-** Say no gracefully and express your desires with a firm yet kind tone.
3. **Embrace the power of silence-** A well-timed pause can be more powerful than a word salad.

Remember, assertive communication is the foundation for vibrant connections and a life where you transform from feeling invisible to feeling unstoppable. So, drop the invisibility cloak personally and professionally and unleash your inner lioness. The world needs to hear your roar!

Unlock the Power of "I": Secrets to Assertive Communication

1. Know Your Rights

The foundation of assertiveness is understanding your right to think, feel, and express yourself, set boundaries, and make your own choices. It is not being pushy or disrespectful, but recognizing your inherent right to be heard and that you matter exactly as you are.

2. Identify Your Needs and Wants

Before you can communicate assertively, you must be clear on what you need and want, what you will do, and what you will not. Take time to reflect on your feelings and the desired result. Other people are not mind-readers and will not always intuitively know what you need or want. Self-Responsability also means communicating your needs so others clearly understand your expectations and desired outcomes.

3. Use "I" Statements

"I" statements are a powerful tool for assertive communication. They focus on your feelings and experiences, avoiding blame and accusatory language. You statements often create more friction than solutions.

"I think....."

"I feel......."

"I need to ....." "I need you to...."

"I want to....."

Example: "Ugh, you never clean up your side of the room! It's a mess!"

"I feel stressed when the living space is cluttered. Would you be open to setting up a cleaning schedule together?"

4. Maintain Confident Body Language

The unspoken conversation: nonverbal cues can make or break the impact of our words. Make eye contact, stand tall with an open posture, and speak in a clear, firm voice. When you are in alignment with your values, beliefs, emotions, and actions, your body language will automatically respond to your inner being of confidence. You do not have to fake it until you make it, pretending to be something you're not because the strength will already be activated within you.

5. Active Listening

Active listening is a key part of assertive communication. It isn't just about speaking but listening attentively to others to gain clarity and understanding. When you truly understand another person's perspective, you can respond more effectively and collaboratively.

- **Give full attention:** Make eye contact, put away distractions (phones!), and show you're engaged with the speaker's body language.

- **Reflect and paraphrase:** Briefly rephrase what you heard to show understanding. "So what you're saying is..."

- **Use nonverbal cues to show you're following along.** Nodding, smiling appropriately, and furrowed brows (when appropriate) can all signal understanding

- **Ask clarifying questions:** Don't interrupt, but ask open-ended questions to gain clarity. "Can you elaborate on that point?"

- **Summarize key points:** Periodically summarize the conversation to ensure you're on the same page.

- **Instead of:** "That's a terrible idea!" **Try:** "I hear your frustration with this approach. Can you tell me more about what concerns you?" Ask questions to clarify what you heard and ensure you understand what was said. Open-ended questions are great for gaining a broader understanding, while closed-ended questions help confirm specifics.

Open-Ended Questions
Elicit more information

- "It sounds like something might be on your mind. Would you like to share what's worrying you?

- What do you mean by...?"

- "I'm curious, how did you arrive at that conclusion?"

- **Encourage elaboration**

- "Can you elaborate on that point?"

- "What does that look like in practice?"

- "Could you give me an example?"

- **Seek deeper understanding**"So, what you're saying is...?" (paraphrase to confirm understanding)"How does this connect to...?""What are the implications of that?"

Closed-Ended Questions

- **Confirm specific details**

- "Is that a 9:00 am meeting or a pm meeting?"

- "Did you say Tuesday or Wednesday?"

- "Was it the blue or black pen you preferred?"

- **Verify assumptions**

- "So, you're interested in going with option A?"

- "Are there any alternative perspectives we should consider before moving forward?"

- "Are we on the same page here?"

6. Practice Saying No

Saying no is a crucial aspect of assertiveness. It empowers you to set boundaries and prioritize your needs. Practice saying no politely but firmly, with a clear explanation if necessary. (We will explore this more in the next chapter)

7. Use Positive Language

Focus on solutions rather than dwelling on problems. Frame your requests positively, suggesting alternatives or compromises when possible.

8. Be Respectful, Even When Disagreeing

You can be assertive while still being respectful of others' opinions. Disagree with ideas, not people.

9. Don't Be Afraid of Silence

It is perfectly acceptable to allow a pause in the conversation. Sometimes, a well-timed silence can be a powerful tool for emphasizing your point. It also shows respect, giving the other person time to think about what you just said.

10. Practice Makes Progress

Developing assertive communication takes time and practice. Role-play with friends or family, and gradually incorporate these skills into your daily interactions.

Assertiveness is a communication skill, not a personality trait. Celebrate your achievements, big or small, to fuel the fire within and keep you motivated on your journey. After all, mastering any skill takes time and practice.

These foundations you are learning will prepare you to be ready to put assertive communication into action. Chapter 4 dives into the real world, equipping you with specific strategies for saying no in different situations. Remember, mastering the art of no is a strategy to building stronger connections, navigating challenges confidently, and ultimately living a fulfilling life.

Chapter 4: The Art Of "Simple No" Strategy: Setting Boundaries

"We may encounter many defeats but we must not be defeated." - Maya Angelou, Poet, Activist

*****

From Messy Kitchen to Masterpiece: The Power of Confidence

A storm raged outside Maya's bakery as she meticulously decorated a wedding cake. Suddenly, a booming voice shattered the calm. Harold, a feared food critic, barged in. He was a notorious food critic known for his scathing reviews.

Harold sneered at the bakery. "This doesn't scream high-profile wedding cake," he boomed. "Let me see the kitchen."

Panic flickered in Maya's usually calm eyes. The kitchen was a disaster, yet she straightened. Harold was trying to bully her, and she would not allow it. "No" she said, her voice surprisingly firm.

Harold sputtered. "No? You can't deny a critic access to the—"

"This isn't about a critic," Maya interrupted, her gaze steady. "This is about respecting my workspace. The kitchen is currently unavailable, and the cake speaks for itself."

Harold, stunned by her calm defiance, stammered. He eyed the cake, a masterpiece of delicate sugar flowers and swirling buttercream. A grudging respect flickered in his eyes.

"Alright, alright," he muttered, backing down. "Show me the cake, then."

Maya smiled, a hint of steel in it. She led him to the cake, explaining her choices with quiet confidence.

Harold, surprisingly subdued, listened intently. Later, when his review came out, it was surprisingly positive, praising the "unexpected gem" and the baker's "unwavering dedication to her craft."

Maya, reading the review, couldn't help but smile. A simple "no" had not only protected her space but also earned her respect.

*****

No Apologies: Why a Simple "No" Empowers Resilience

Have you ever felt like your time is a bottomless well, constantly being dipped into by the requests of others? Is the endless "yes" wearing you out and making you long for a break? One straightforward yet frequently under-appreciated word holds the key to taking back control of your life and developing radiant resilience: **no**. But why is a simple "no" so powerful?

The Power of the Immediate Halt: A clear and confident "no" acts as an immediate stop sign, closing the door on further discussion. This allows you to maintain control of the situation and steer the conversation in the direction you want it to go.

Justification Opens the Door for Negotiation: While the urge to offer justifications or lengthy explanations for your decisions may be strong, resist it! Justifications are like tempting pastries in a bakery window for those who want to pick apart your boundaries.

Consider this example: Imagine Maya, a baker, is busy fulfilling an order when a customer, Harold, asks for a sneak peek of her kitchen. If Maya had replied, "Well, the kitchen is a bit chaotic right now because I'm finishing another order, but maybe after I clean up a bit, you could take a quick peek?" the outcome could have been quite different.

Conditions Weaken the "No": By mentioning "maybe" and a "quick peek" later, Maya opens the door for negotiation. Harold might argue or pressure her into letting him in now since he's there. This weakens her initial "no" and could lead to further requests or criticisms.

Respect Begets Respect: When you confidently assert your boundaries with a simple "no," you elevate your value. You demonstrate to others that your time and energy cannot be taken for granted. This, in turn, commands respect from those around you, even a critic like Harold.

Body Language Speaks Volumes: Your Secret Weapon for Powerful Communication

Have you ever walked into a room and suddenly felt the energy change? Or maybe you've met someone whose handshake was limp with sweaty palms that left a lasting impression on you about this person? That's the power of body language. It is the silent conversation that happens alongside our spoken words, and it can often reveal more about a person than anything they could say. Confident body language and a firm tone are your armor when saying 'no.' They transform a hesitant 'maybe later' into a resolute 'no' that demands respect.

Confidence from the Inside Out: 6 Ways Body Language Transforms You:

1) **The First Impression Advantage:** Body language sets the tone for every interaction. Confident posture, eye contact, and a genuine smile create a positive first impression, while crossed arms, fidgeting, and a frown can make you seem closed off, nervous, or unapproachable.

2) **Beyond Words:** Our body language can convey emotions we might be trying to hide. A forced smile or clenched jaw can betray our true feelings, while open gestures and relaxed posture can communicate openness and trust.

3) **Power Projection:** Confident body language doesn't just affect how others perceive you, it can also impact how you perceive yourself. Standing tall and making eye contact can boost your confidence and give you an edge over any situation.

4) **Active Listening:** Body language isn't a one-way street. Actively listening with open body posture, leaning in slightly, and maintaining eye contact shows the speaker you're engaged and interested in what they say.

5) **Creating a Boundary:** Confident body language, like maintaining a comfortable distance and using open palms, establishes a clear boundary. It tells the other person you are not open to negotiation.

6) **Nonverbal "No":** Strong body language can be enough on its own. A raised eyebrow or a firm shake of the head, coupled with eye contact, can silently but effectively communicate your refusal.

Confident Tone: The Soundtrack to Your Success Story

Think of a presentation or standup comedian that really captivated you and drew you in, not just with their content, but their voice. That is the power of a confident tone. It is the melody that carries your message, transforming it from mere words into a compelling call to action.

Here's why mastering a confident tone is crucial for anyone who wants to be a champion for their ideas and master the skills of having radiant resilience:

- **Leaves No Room for Debate:** A firm, clear voice leaves no room for misinterpretation. Avoid hesitant tones or rising inflections that might sound like a question. Speak confidently and directly, using strong verbs like "decline" or "cannot.

- **Commands Respect:** A confident tone demands respect for your decision. It shows you are serious, know the value of your time and energy, and won't be easily pressured.

- **Maintains Professionalism:** Even when saying "no," a professional tone is crucial. This doesn't mean being harsh, but it ensures your message is delivered with courtesy and respect, even if the answer is firm.

Society plays a significant role in how women experience the fear of saying no. The "fear of what other people think," often referred to as social anxiety, is a feeling of apprehension or worry when you anticipate that others are about to judge, criticize or disapprove of you. The stereotype that women are bad at conflict can make them hesitant to say no for fear of causing a scene or being seen as difficult. This fear can stem from low self-esteem or a lack of confidence in your abilities.

It's important to note, that some degree of concern about social evaluation is natural. We are social creatures who crave connection and acceptance. If this fear becomes excessive, it can creep into your daily life, disrupting decision-making and time management. When you fixate on others' opinions and judgments, you risk losing sight of your own identity, true nature, and purpose. This constant pressure can pull you away from your authentic path.

Studies show that the number one cause of stress on a regular daily basis is dealing with negative people. Critics are everywhere and can be a real thorn in your side, personally and professionally.

Friend or Foe? Decoding the 3 Faces of Criticism

1. **The Knowledgeable Critic:** These critics offer constructive feedback to help you improve based on their expertise and understanding of the subject matter. They give specific suggestions and insights to transform your work to the next level. There is much to be gained from this type of information. These critics are open to you asking for clarification about their feedback to gain further insight on how to improve your craft and build confidence.

2. **The Negative Critic:** These critics focus on tearing you down rather than offering helpful advice and their primary objective is to find fault. Their criticism is harsh, judgmental, and often lacks justification. It's designed to belittle, invalidate, and discourage you, not to help you grow. Sometimes, Negative Critics resort to personal attacks, criticizing you or your character instead of focusing on the work. Don't take their negativity personally. Limit your interaction and focus on those who uplift you.

3. **The Attention Seeker:** These critics crave a reaction and want to get you flustered, defensive, or even angry. Their need for attention might stem from insecurity or a desire to feel validated. By criticizing you, they might be trying to boost their own ego and make themselves better than they are. Don't give them the satisfaction of bringing you down and playing in their arena. How they view themselves or the world around them is not your responsibility or your business and the only thing you can control is what you think and how you respond to their behavior. The best response is to ignore them or respond with "Thank you for your feedback" and get on with your life.

Critique Check: From Sting to Success: 6 Steps to Turn Criticism into Your Ally

Discernment is a valuable skill in all aspects of life, particularly when dealing with negative input that could pull you off your path. It empowers you to navigate challenges by carefully evaluating situations, making informed choices even in difficult circumstances, choosing healthy relationships, and avoiding toxic situations. Ultimately, discernment helps you live a fulfilling life by recognizing true value and quality.

Here are 6 easy steps to perform a "Critique Check" and separate the gold from the garbage in any feedback you receive:

1. **Stay Calm:** Don't get defensive or angry. It's all just information until you give it meaning. Take a deep breath and assess the situation.
2. **Evaluate the Intent:** Is this constructive criticism or negativity disguised as feedback?
3. **Consider the Source:** Does this person's opinion hold weight? Is it in line with your core values? Does it support your goals and desired outcomes?
4. **Filter the Feedback:** Not all criticism is valid. There are lots of people who like to give unsolicited advice. Take what's useful and leave the rest.
5. **Respond with Confidence:** If you choose to respond, do so calmly and clearly. Explain your position or state your disagreement using the "I" statements suggested previously.
6. **Focus on Your Goals:** Don't let critics distract you from your path and throw you off your game. There is no need to carry around the negativity all day from a passing negative moment.

We've established the power of a simple "no," but a pending concern might be: "How do I say no politely without seeming rude or inconsiderate?" The fear of appearing rude stems from a desire to be considerate of others' feelings. However, saying yes to everything can be inconsiderate to yourself in the long run, leading to resentment or burnout.

You must also consider your feelings, energy levels, and available resources. When other people are pushing boundaries and attempting to cross lines, it is imperative that you use this strategy for saying no to maintain control of a situation and not get buried in something you may not be able to handle later on.

When a request is too much, a simple "no" is best. Some illustrations of this include:

- **Unreasonable Request**

- Taking on an impossible workload with an unrealistic deadline.

- Lending a large sum of money you can't afford.

- Participating in an activity that violates your morals or safety.

- **Unsolicited Advice**

- When someone offers unsolicited advice, especially in a critical way, a simple "no" can shut down the conversation. You can follow with, "Thank you, but I'll handle this myself."

- **High-Pressure Sales Tactics**

- When a salesperson uses pressure tactics to force a sale, a simple "no, thank you" and a firm exit strategy are your best weapons.

- **If someone rudely interrupts you**

- a direct "no" reclaims your right to speak and sets a boundary.

Following Through on a Previous "No": If you've already declined a request and the person keeps pressuring you, a simple "no, I already said that" is firm and avoids further discussion.

The "No" Zone: Mastering Your Boundaries at Work, Home, and Everywhere In Between

Unrealistic Deadlines

- Client: "We need the final design by the end of the day, no exceptions." (It's a complex project)

- You (firmly): "No, while I understand the urgency, a rushed job might compromise quality. A realistic deadline would be [suggest a date]."

Unwanted Social Activities

- Friend: "Hey, want to come with us to that heavy metal concert tonight?" (You hate heavy metal)

- You (with a smile):"No, thanks. Not really my scene, but have fun!"

Saying No to Family

- Sibling: "Can you lend me some money? I need it for [reason]."

- You (lovingly): "No, I'm tight on finances right now. Perhaps we can brainstorm some ways for you to earn some extra cash?"

Saying NO To Your Spouse

- Spouse: "Hey Honey, Jimmy's surprise party is tonight at 8:00 pm. Do you want to go?"

- You: "No, honey. I appreciate you thinking of me, but honestly, I'm beat after this week. A night in with some takeout sounds amazing right now."

We've just whipped up a perfect "no" – firm yet light, delivered with the confidence of a master chef. A simple "no" uttered with strength is not a sign of weakness but a declaration of empowerment that takes courage. You are the sovereign of your time, energy, and resources. Your "no" is a decree, not a suggestion. Sometimes, a simple smile can soften the direct approach of a "no" while maintaining firmness. It shows you're not being rude or unpleasant, just assertive. In Chapter 5, we'll learn the art of the "Thank You, But No Thanks." It's like adding a touch of sweetness to your "no," showing appreciation while keeping your boundaries firm.

Chapter 5: The Art Of "Thank You, But No Thanks" Strategy: Reduce Guilt

"The future belongs to those who believe in the beauty of their dreams." - Eleanor Roosevelt, Former First Lady of the United States

*****

Following Your Compass: Saying No to Cruises, Charting a Course for Passion

The life of a freelance writer, like a well-crafted sentence, requires a balance of structure and flexibility. Yet, maintaining that balance can be challenging, especially when faced with an overflowing inbox of requests. Enter the "Thank You, But No Thanks," a powerful yet polite tool that allows us to gracefully decline projects while preserving our professional reputation and fostering continued collaboration in relationships.

Breanna's evocative prose and eye for detail had landed her a loyal readership and a growing roster of potential clients. She is a rising star in the world of travel writing. But with each new inquiry, Breanna faced the delicate dance of saying "yes" to the projects that ignited her passion, while politely declining those that strayed from her chosen niche.

While sipping her morning coffee, Breanna reviewed her inbox when a particular email caught her attention from a prominent travel magazine. Breanna had worked on projects for them in the past when she first started freelancing and knew they offered some pretty luxurious job opportunities.

The editor, Ms. Davies, offered Maya an exciting opportunity: a week-long cruise to the Caribbean, all expenses paid, in exchange for a series of articles. While Breanna adored the Caribbean's vibrant culture and turquoise waters, her expertise lay in exploring lesser-known destinations, delving into their hidden gems and authentic experiences. A luxury cruise, with its regimented itinerary and focus on high-end amenities, didn't resonate with her writing style or target audience.

Breanna considered the pros and cons of taking this opportunity, as well as her current lifestyle, passions, and interests. She had many check marks in favor of the job offer but when Breanna measured it against her core values, she got a sinking feeling in her stomach. The job didn't feel right. One of her top core values was exploring/adventure. Breanna knew her creativity would be stifled and she would not be able to produce her best work for the magazine or their readership.

*****

Building Bridges: From "No" to Future Opportunities

Here's how Breanna crafted her "Thank You, But No Thanks" with the utmost professionalism:

"Dear Ms. Davies,"

"Thank you so much for reaching out and offering this incredible opportunity to travel to the Caribbean. I'm truly honoured to be considered for such a prestigious assignment."

"While exploring the Caribbean holds immense appeal, my writing typically focuses on uncovering the unique charm of less-traveled destinations, providing readers with a deeper understanding of local culture and off-the-beaten-path experiences. My strengths are highlighting hidden gems and fostering a sense of adventure."

"However, I would be delighted to discuss potential future collaborations that align more closely with my expertise. Perhaps a piece on sustainable travel practices in Southeast Asia, or a series exploring the historical wonders of Eastern Europe? I'd be happy to connect and brainstorm some ideas that would be a perfect fit for both your audience and my writing style."

By acknowledging the offer's appeal, explaining her focus, and proposing alternative collaborations, Breanna politely declines the cruise project while leaving the door open for future opportunities. This approach strengthens her professional relationship with Ms. Davies, showcasing her expertise and commitment to her niche.

The "Thank You, But No Thanks," wielded with respect and clarity, allows us to navigate the sometimes turbulent waters of freelance life. By mastering this art, we can build strong professional relationships, curate our creative output, and ensure a successful – and fulfilling – writing journey.

The Right Fit Formula: Skills + Values + Lifestyle = Career Fulfillment

Breanna's story illustrates a dream career as a perfectly crafted puzzle. The pieces, each representing a crucial element, need to fit together seamlessly to create a picture of satisfaction and fulfillment. It also illustrates how there could be variety and many options within a chosen field.

Here's a breakdown of the three elements (Skills, Values, and Lifestyle) and their importance in aligning your career:

1. Skills

- **Definition:** These are your talents, abilities, and acquired knowledge. Skills can be technical (software proficiency, data analysis), creative (writing, design), or interpersonal (communication, teamwork).

- **Importance:** Your skills are the foundation of your career path. Choosing a field that utilizes your strengths and allows you to develop new skills keeps you engaged, motivated, and competitive.

2. Values

- **Definition:** These are your core principles and beliefs that guide your decision-making. Values can be related to work ethic (integrity, innovation), work environment (collaboration, autonomy), or purpose (social impact, financial security).

- **Importance:** Aligning your career with your values fosters a sense of fulfillment and authenticity. Working in a role that contradicts your values can lead to frustration and burnout.

3. Lifestyle

- **Definition:** This refers to your desired work-life balance and personal aspirations. Lifestyle considerations include travel frequency, work schedule flexibility, and income potential.

- **Importance:** Understanding your ideal lifestyle helps you choose a career path that allows you to achieve your personal goals. A demanding career that requires constant travel might not be compatible with someone who prioritizes spending time with family.

How They Work Together:

These three elements intertwine to create a holistic picture of your ideal career.

- **Skills** are the tools you bring to the table.

- **Values** guide where you want to use those tools.

- **Lifestyle** defines the work environment and schedule that aligns with your overall well-being.

When considering all three elements, you can make informed career decisions that ensure you thrive in your purpose, passion, professional satisfaction, and personal fulfillment.

Mastering the Art of "Thank You, But No Thanks" at Work

The Overloaded Calendar

- **Situation:** You're a marketing manager with a full schedule. A colleague approaches you about taking on some social media management tasks for a new client.

- **Curator Approach:** "Thank you for thinking of me, [colleague's name]! I truly appreciate the offer. Right now, my exhibition (career) is already showcasing a diverse range of marketing campaigns (projects). To ensure each piece gets the attention it deserves (maintain high-quality work), I wouldn't be able to dedicate the time needed to manage the social media aspect for this new client. However, I'd be happy to connect you with some social media specialists in my network who might be a great fit for this project."

The Networking Event

- **Situation:** You're attending a networking event and someone offers to connect you with someone in their network for a job opportunity that doesn't align with your career goals.

- **Compass Approach:** "Thank you so much for the offer to connect me, [name]! I truly appreciate it. My career compass (values and goals) is pointing me toward [mention your desired career path]. While the opportunity you mentioned sounds interesting, it wouldn't be the best fit for my long-term goals. However, if you ever come across opportunities in the [mention your desired field] realm, I'd love to be connected!"

Empowering Your "Yes" with Effective "No": A Guide to Decision-Making

Saying "no" to an opportunity can feel daunting, but it empowers you to focus on projects that ignite your passion. Here's a framework to navigate choices and make confident decisions:

1. Clarity of Purpose:(with a Self-Care Twist)

- **Action Step:** Define your career goals, considering not just "what" you want to achieve, but also "how" you want to achieve it.

- **Tip:** Ask yourself not only "What kind of impact do I want to make?" but also "What work environment allows me to feel energized and fulfilled?"

- **Self-Care Integration:** Visualizing your dream career should not only involve the projects you want to work on but also the work-life balance and overall well-being you desire.

Example: Instead of just picturing yourself writing articles for a travel magazine, imagine yourself working flexible hours, with time for exploration and travel built into your schedule. This allows you to see how your career goals align with your need for a healthy work-life balance.

2. Values Check (with a Self-Care Focus):

- **Action Step:** Identify your core values, including not just those related directly to work, but also those that contribute to your overall well-being.

- **Tip:** Expand your values list to include things like "work-life balance," "mental health," "creativity," and "personal growth."

- **Self-Care Integration:**Consider how your career choices will impact your ability to prioritize your core values. Does this opportunity allow you to maintain a healthy work-life balance and have time for activities that nourish your mental and physical well-being?

Example: If "creativity" is a core value for you, saying no to a project with rigid guidelines might be the self-care choice, even if it seems like a good opportunity.

3. Feasibility Check (with a Self-Care Lens):

- **Action Step:** Be honest about your bandwidth, considering not just your workload but also your energy levels and emotional well-being.

- **Tip:** When considering the project's deadlines, ask yourself if meeting them will lead to overwhelm resulting in no time for personal activities that recharge your batteries.

- **Self-Care Integration:** Taking on too much is detrimental to your health and impacts your overall productivity. Saying no to a project can be a form of self-care, allowing you to focus on existing commitments by scheduling time for your rest and social life.

Example: If you're already overwhelmed, taking on a new project might not be the best decision for your well-being, even if it seems like a good opportunity.

By weaving self-care principles into each step of the decision-making framework, you can ensure that your career choices not only align with your goals but also contribute to your overall well-being and sense of fulfillment.

4. Long-Term Vision:

- **Action Step:** Evaluate the long-term implications. Does this opportunity align with your overall career goals?

- **Tip:** Consider if the project offers learning opportunities, builds your network, or leads to future projects that resonate more with your goals.

5. Positive Impact:

• **Action Step:** Think beyond yourself. Who might benefit from you saying "no" to this opportunity?

• **Tip:** Saying "no" allows you to focus on existing commitments or frees you to pursue other opportunities that might benefit a wider audience or group. It's about making choices that maximize your positive impact.

By integrating these steps, you can transform your "no"s into empowered decisions that propel you toward a fulfilling career. This decision process will work with making decisions about family and personal life choices as well. Remember, saying "no" doesn't mean missing out on opportunities, it means making space for the "yes" that aligns with your passions and goals.

Setting Boundaries with Grace: The "Thank You, But No Thanks" Approach for Family

Here are some ways to use the "Thank You, But No Thanks" approach to politely decline requests from family while still maintaining positive relationships:

Express Gratitude and Appreciation:

- Start by acknowledging their request and expressing your appreciation for them thinking of you.

- "Thank you so much for inviting me to [event/gathering]. I appreciate you wanting me to be there."

Explain Your Limits:

- Be clear and honest about why you can't participate.

- You can use phrases like:

- "Unfortunately, I already have a prior commitment that evening."

- "I'm feeling a bit overwhelmed this week and need some time to recharge."

- "With everything going on right now, I just wouldn't be able to give it my full attention."

Offer Alternatives (Optional):

- If possible, suggest an alternative way you can connect.
- "Maybe we can get together for lunch next week instead?"
- "I'd love to hear all about it when you return."

Focus on Shared Values (Optional):

• Frame your response around values you share with your family, like family time or self-care.

• "Spending quality time with the family is important to me, and I want to make sure I'm fully present when we do get together."

• "Taking care of myself allows me to be more present for everyone else in the long run."

Examples:

• **Scenario:** You're swamped with work and your family wants you to help with a big family reunion.

• "Thanks so much for including me in the reunion plans! I know how much effort goes into these events. Unfortunately, with everything going on at work right now, I wouldn't be able to contribute as much as I'd like and I need to sit this out. I'd love to hear all about it when you get back."

• **Scenario:** Your in-laws want you to come over every weekend, but you need some personal time.

• "I always love spending time with you guys, and I appreciate the invitations. This weekend, I need to catch up on some reading and relax a bit. Would it be okay if we planned to get together next weekend instead? Maybe we could try that new restaurant you mentioned?"

• **Scenario:** Your sibling asks you to babysit their kids on short notice, but you have a prior commitment.

• "Thanks for thinking of me to watch the kids! Unfortunately, I already have a [mention your prior commitment] that evening. You could call (name) and see if they are available."

Remember, the key is to be honest, clear, and kind. By expressing your appreciation and offering solutions when possible, you can maintain strong family relationships even when you have to say no.

Beyond the Checklist: Creative Strategies For Fulfilling Your Dreams

Creativity plays a vital role in decision-making by offering a broader perspective and fostering innovative solutions. Here's how it empowers you to make effective choices:

Finding Unconventional Solutions:

- Creativity allows you to break free from traditional thinking and consider solutions that might not have been readily apparent. This can lead to breakthrough ideas that address the core of a problem more effectively.

- Overcoming challenges when faced with roadblocks or unexpected difficulties, creativity helps you find alternative pathways to reach your desired outcome. It equips you with the resourcefulness to navigate complexities.

- Many ideas on your whole life list can be fulfilled in different ways. Hobbies can become a small business or additional source of income, careers can become travel opportunities, charity/volunteer opportunities can often fulfill opportunities to attend exciting events and meet interesting people, etc.

From Dream List to Desert Dunes: Embracing Adventure with a "Thank You, But No Thanks"

In 2019, I had a "life list" of activities I wanted to experience and places I wanted to go. I am an outdoor/wilderness enthusiast and love courageous adventures. I started researching Egypt when I kept getting visions and having dreams about being there. I had been practising Reiki for several years and learned Egyptian Reiki as well. I couldn't determine why I needed to go to Egypt but the feeling persisted.

One day my Mom said, "You keep talking about this, I think you need to go." The trip was going to be expensive and I had some uncertainty about how I was going to pay for it.

There were lots of people in my circle who were interested in Egypt but only one friend who would possibly go all-in and be up for the kind of adventures I was planning. I decided I would commit to myself and go no matter what, even if meant starting the trip alone and meeting new people along the way.

After figuring out all the details, I called my friend Jules and asked if she wanted to go. She was shocked that this conversation was happening since we casually talked about Egypt many times as a "dream" that we would love to do "someday" but never really expected it to become a reality.

She said she needed to talk to her boyfriend Dennis and figure out some details, could she get back to me the next day with her decision? Half an hour later, Jules called back and said "Yes."

2 days later, I sat at the table in a state of absolute awe looking at my laptop as I booked the itinerary and final details:

- 5 days Nile Cruise,
- hot air balloon ride at sunrise over Luxor,
- 3 days 2 nights camping in the Black & White deserts
- 2 days in Cairo at the pyramids, museums, riding camels, and shopping.

Three major items on my life list were being fulfilled all at once, on the other side of the world in Egypt of all places. Jules offered an additional option to go from Cairo to Ireland for 5 more days and a place to stay with her relatives. I declined with a grateful "thank you but no thank you" since I had to return to work and didn't have the financial resources for the extended trip.

*****

The "Thank You, But No Thanks" approach empowers you to gracefully decline opportunities that don't quite fit, but what about situations where a project completely clashes with your values or career vision? Imagine a dream collaboration offered by a company known for unethical practices, or a high-paying freelance gig that requires skills outside your expertise and detracts from your passion. In these scenarios, a more direct approach is necessary.

Chapter 6 delves into the "This Doesn't Meet My Needs Right Now" strategy, equipping you with the language and confidence to navigate these situations assertively. This approach ensures you attract projects and opportunities that resonate with your vision and empower you to build a fulfilling life.

Chapter 6: The Art Of "This Doesn't Meet My Needs Right Now" Strategy: Set Realistic Expectations

"You are not obligated to win. You are obligated to keep trying. To the best you can every day." - Marian Wright Edelman, Activist

*****

The Ethical Dilemma: Can You Code Your Values?

Sarah, a web developer known for her expertise in building accessible and user-friendly websites, received an email from a large online retailer, MegaMart. The email offered her a seemingly lucrative contract to develop their new e-commerce platform. Intrigued, Sarah opened the attached proposal.

While the initial details were exciting, a sense of unease settled upon her as she delved deeper. The project timeline was aggressively tight, demanding long hours and potentially compromising her commitment to high-quality code. Additionally, the proposal mentioned a proprietary content management system (CMS) known for its clunky interface and accessibility issues.

This clashed directly with Sarah's core values of user experience and accessibility for her clients. A simple "Thank You, But No Thanks" wouldn't be enough. She needed to be clear and upfront about the reasons for declining.

*****

Honesty and Expertise: Sarah Navigates a Misaligned Opportunity Through Email

Taking a deep breath, Sarah opened her email client and crafted a response utilizing the "This Doesn't Meet My Needs Right Now" strategy:

Dear [Hiring Manager name],

Thank you for reaching out and offering the opportunity to work on MegaMart's new e-commerce platform. I was particularly excited about [mention a positive aspect of the proposal].

However, after carefully reviewing the details, I realized that the project's timeline and specific CMS requirements wouldn't allow me to deliver the high-quality, user-friendly experience I strive for. My focus lies in creating accessible and user-friendly websites that prioritize the needs of all visitors.

While this project doesn't align with my expertise, I'd be thrilled to connect with you again in the future if any opportunities arise that better suit my skill set and commitment to accessibility. In the meantime, I wish you all the best in finding the perfect developer for MegaMart's platform.

Sincerely,

Sarah

*****

This response achieved several things. It acknowledged the opportunity's appeal, expressed her core values, and offered a polite "no" while leaving the door open for future collaboration. By utilizing the "This Doesn't Meet My Needs Right Now" strategy, Sarah preserved her professional reputation and remained true to her values while confidently navigating a potentially challenging situation.

Negotiating for Success: Addressing Deadlines and Skill Mismatches

This strategy can be a powerful tool for managing your time, allowing you to focus on tasks that truly matter and avoid feeling overwhelmed. Here's when to implement it:

Overloaded with Work

- "This additional project doesn't meet my current priorities. However, I can review it after I complete [existing project] in [time frame]."

Unrealistic Deadline

- "Unfortunately, this deadline doesn't meet my current capacity. Is there any flexibility to adjust it to [more realistic time frame]?"

Task Doesn't Align with Skills

- "While I appreciate the offer, my expertise isn't suited for this specific task. Perhaps [colleague] with their background in [relevant skill] would be a better fit."

Saying No with Love: Mastering the Art of Gentle Boundaries in Family

This strategy can be adapted for family situations. It will require a touch of warmth and understanding to navigate the emotional dynamics since it can come off as harsh or uncaring.

Softening the Tone

- Replace "Needs" with "Capacity": "This doesn't fit my capacity right now" sounds gentler and allows for future possibilities.

- Acknowledge and Appreciate: Show empathy! Start by acknowledging the importance of spending time together. For example, you could say, "Spending quality time with you is important to me, and I appreciate you wanting to [activity]."

● Offer Alternatives: "I can't [unwanted activity], but I would love to [alternative activity] together."

By implementing the "This Doesn't Meet My Needs Right Now" strategy, you control your schedule and free up valuable time to focus on your most important tasks. This allows you to be more productive, achieve your desires and outcomes faster, and reduce stress and overwhelm. Effective life management strategies involve planning, organization, and prioritization.

Design Your Ideal Life: Define What You Truly Desire: Unleash Your Inner Visionary

1. Goal Setting and Prioritization:

• **Define Your Desired Outcomes Daily:** Start by setting a clear end result that you want to achieve. "I choose the end result of.........."

• **Consider what you want to accomplish personally and professionally:** When creating a life you love, it is important that the end result you desire is for no other reason than you would love it. Ask yourself, "Why do I want this?" "What will having this end result give me?" "How will I feel when I have this result?" If your end result is to satisfy someone else, or because you think the goal will solve one of the 6 Negative Thinking patterns, your end result is coming from your unconscious. This will shift the power outside of you and will not satisfy you emotionally. Only a true choice from your heart's desire will empower.

• **Consider both long-term and short-term desire:** What results do you want to accomplish in your personal and professional life? These become your daily/weekly/monthly activities. It is important to visualize yourself achieving the end result and get into the emotion of having it.

• **Prioritize ruthlessly:** Not all tasks are created equal. Identify the most important tasks (those that contribute most to your desired end result) and prioritize them to be done first when you have the most mental capacity available. Lesser tasks or tasks that are relaxing to wind down can be scheduled later that don't require as much mental capacity.

2. Planning and Scheduling:

- **Create a "Get To Do" List:** There are certain tasks that we have to do but equally important are the things we "get to do" that are simply for pure pleasure and enjoyment. Make sure to write these in your agenda or journal as confirmation to your brain that fun and pleasure are also priorities in your life with the people you love. This also helps create mental/emotional space between work and personal life.

- "I get to spend time with my kids for movie night."

- "I get to go on a date with my spouse/partner on Friday night"

- "I get to cheer on my favorite team at the game"

- **Schedule Your Activities:** Consider using tools like planners, project management apps, or time trackers to manage your schedule and deadlines effectively. Delegate time slots in your calendar for specific activities, meetings, appointments, working out at the gym, meditation, and time with friends/family. This creates a visual representation of your day and helps you stay on track.

3. Focus and Avoiding Distractions:

- **Minimize Multitasking:** Multitasking is a distraction to your brain that decreases productivity and has the potential for important tasks to be left incomplete, leading to increased stress. Focus on completing one task at a time to achieve higher-quality results in a shorter time frame.

- **Minimize Distractions:** Silence notifications, turn off your phone during focused work periods, and find a quiet space to minimize interruptions.

4. Delegation and Time Management:

- **Delegate Tasks:** Don't be afraid to delegate tasks that can be handled by others. This frees up valuable time for you to focus on your core competencies.

- **Learn to Say No:** The "This Doesn't Meet My Needs Right Now" strategy, as discussed previously, empowers you to politely decline requests that don't align with your priorities or schedule.

5. Self-Care and Time Management:

- **Schedule Breaks:** Strategically planned breaks have enormous potential for improved brain function. Science has proven that taking short breaks and making time to practise relaxed breathing calms your nervous system, diminishing stress that could lead to overwhelm

- **Maintain a Healthy Lifestyle:** Prioritize adequate sleep, healthy eating, and regular exercise. A healthy body and mind are essential for optimal productivity and time management.

Remember: The best time management strategy is the one that works for you. Experiment with different techniques and find a system that helps you be most productive and achieve your goals with less stress and overwhelm.

In her book "Atlas of the Heart," Brene Brown brilliantly describes the differences in stress levels as follows:

"**Stressed-** is like being in the weeds,

- when the cognitive brain starts thinking the environmental demand is beyond your ability to cope.

- Emotions do not come from the body feeling stress, this is a myth. Our emotions are responding to the thinking assessment from the brain, I can't handle it, this is too much.

Overwhelmed- is like being blown. The definition of overwhelm is an extreme level of stress, an emotional or cognitive intensity to the point of feeling unable to function.

- Overwhelm happens when Life events are unfolding faster than my psyche and nervous system can manage it.

- The only way back is to engage in "non-doing" restful activity. This is NOT a time to engage in problem-solving. Research has shown we don't process other emotions or information when we are overwhelmed and this can result in poor decision making."Brown, Brene. Atlas Of The Heart, 2021 Random House

Prioritizing your needs is not selfish, it is essential for thriving. By mastering this strategy, you can confidently manage your time and energy and shine even brighter! In the next chapter, we'll explore the art of offering alternative solutions when a simple "no" might not be the best fit.

As we saw with Sarah's response to MegaMart, a direct and honest approach can be the most effective way to decline a request that doesn't align with your values or workload. But what happens when the situation is a little more complex? Perhaps the request is intriguing, but some aspects raise concerns, or maybe you need more information before you make a decision. In these scenarios, the "This Doesn't Meet My Needs Right Now" strategy might not be the best fit. In Chapter 7, we'll explore the "I Need Time to Think" tactic for navigating these situations effectively.

Chapter 7: The Art Of "I Need Time to Think" Strategy: Taking Control of Your Response

"The best and most beautiful things in the world cannot be seen or even touched - they must be felt with the heart." - Helen Keller, Author, Activist

*****

From Knee-Jerk "No" to Empowered "Yes": A Story of Negotiation and Connection

Dianna slammed the bedroom door with a force that rattled the picture frames on the wall. Her 16-year-old daughter, Nikki, winced from her spot on the bed, headphones blaring. Moments ago, Dianna discovered Nikki's meticulously planned weekend getaway with friends – a two-hour drive away, involving a rickety cabin Dianna had never heard of and chaperoned by a barely-legal college student.

Dianna's initial reaction was a firm, knee-jerk "no" stemming from safety concerns and frustration at Nikki's lack of transparency. However, the memory of her own teenage experience when she was 16 empowered her to pause and seek a solution that addressed both concerns." Her mother had said no initially, a response fueled by her Mother's worry. But then, after a tearful conversation and a revised plan with clear safety measures, her mother had relented.

Taking a deep breath, Dianna knocked on Nikki's door. "Hey, can we talk?" she asked gently. Nikki, expecting another lecture, sighed and pulled out an earbud.

"About this weekend trip," Dianna began, "my first instinct was to say no. But I also know you're growing up, and I want to understand your plans better." Dianna explained her concerns about the cabin and the chaperone.

"I hear you, Mom," Nikki said, surprised by the shift in tone. "The cabin is owned by a family friend, and this other girl's older brother is a responsible guy."

Dianna listened patiently as Nikki elaborated on the plan, the excitement bubbling beneath the surface. Dianna knew an immediate decision wouldn't be productive. "Look," she said, "this sounds like fun, but there are still some details we need to iron out. Why don't you take some time to research the cabin and find out more about this chaperone? Let's talk again tomorrow night, and we can come up with a plan that works for everyone."

The "I Need Time to Think" tactic, while not the immediate answer Nikki craved, opened a space for conversation. The following evening, they discussed the trip in detail. Dianna offered alternatives for the chaperone and suggested they keep her updated throughout the weekend. To Nikki's surprise, Dianna even agreed to help with some of the costs.

The weekend arrived, and Dianna felt a pang of worry as Nikki drove away with her friends. However, this time, it was a worry tempered by trust. Nikki had proven her maturity by taking responsibility for planning the trip, and Dianna, by taking a step back, wasn't just delaying a decision, she was empowering both herself and Nikki to reach a mutually beneficial outcome. When Nikki returned, suntanned and full of stories, the relief and joy on her face solidified Dianna's belief in the power of the pause.

"You know, when you first told me about the trip, I almost said no right away. But taking that time to talk and gather more information helped me understand your plans and feel comfortable saying yes with some boundaries in place." "Thanks, Mom. It meant a lot that you listened and trusted me to be responsible. It made the whole experience even better."

It wasn't about saying no, but about saying yes – to communication, trust, and a growing relationship of love, trust and connection with her daughter.

*****

Calm, Cool, and Collected: The Power of Delay for Savvy Choices

Saying yes or no on the spot can be tempting, especially when emotions run high. However, the "I Need Time to Think" tactic empowers you to take a step back and gain control of the situation. Here's how the power of delay can benefit you:

- **Clearer Thinking:** The initial rush of excitement or pressure can cloud your judgment. Taking a breather allows you to process the information objectively, and identify potential challenges or red flags you might have missed in the heat of the moment, and reflect on what's truly important to you

- **Reduced Stress:** Impulsive decisions often lead to stress and regret later. Hitting the pause button gives you time to calm down and approach the situation from a calmer, more rational perspective.

- **Consider All Options:** Delaying your response allows you to explore alternatives and potential solutions you might not have initially considered. Identify your strengths, weaknesses, time constraints, and budget limitations. This awareness helps you understand what you can realistically achieve or commit to. This can lead to a more creative and mutually beneficial outcome for everyone involved.

- **Gathering Information:** Quite often, more details will be required to make an informed decision. The "I Need Time to Think" tactic allows you to gather additional information, ask clarifying questions, and ensure you have a complete picture before committing or saying no.

- **Prioritized Response:** Sometimes, saying yes to one request means neglecting a higher priority. The power of delay allows you to assess your current commitments and ensure this new request aligns with your overall goals and workload.

Remember: Priorities and limitations are not fixed. They can evolve over time as your circumstances and goals change. Regularly revisiting them will ensure your decisions remain aligned with where you are in life.

When to Use the "I Need Time to Think" Tactic

The "I Need Time to Think" tactic isn't a one-size-fits-all solution, but it can be incredibly beneficial in several key situations:

- Major Decisions: When faced with a life-altering decision, like:

- High-Pressure Situations: When emotions are running high, either yours or the other person's:

- A heated argument

- A negotiation with a pushy salesperson

- A situation where you feel pressured to make a quick decision

- A new job offer with significant changes

- Example: "Thank you for offering me the [position name] position. I'm very interested in learning more about [specific aspect of the job, e.g., benefits package, team structure, etc.]. May I have a day or two to review the offer and ask any clarifying questions before making a decision?"

- A large investment (house, car, etc.)

- Example: "I'd like to take some time to [mention what you need to do next, e.g., discuss the offer with my family/financial advisor, research similar options, review the details of the offer]. Would it be alright if I got back to you by [date] with my decision?"

• A major life change (marriage, relocation,)

It's perfectly acceptable to ask for time. You are not obligated to give an immediate answer, especially for significant purchases or complex requests. The "I Need Time to Think" tactic allows you to gather additional information, ask clarifying questions, and ensure you have a complete picture before committing.

By strategically using the "I Need Time to Think" tactic, you can navigate challenging situations with more confidence and control. Remember, a thoughtful "yes" or a well-reasoned "no" is always better than a rushed decision with regret later.

The Art of Saying No: Empowering Yourself Without Regret

The stereotype that women have a harder time making decisions is a complex issue with social and psychological factors at play. Here's a breakdown of why this stereotype exists and how you can overcome it:

Social Conditioning

- **Pleasing Others:** Women are often socialized to prioritize the needs and feelings of others. This can stem from a desire to be liked or a fear of disappointing others. This can lead to difficulty asserting their own desires and opinions when making decisions.

- Example: A woman facing pressure to attend a social event she doesn't enjoy could explain, "Thank you for the invite! I'd love to consider it. Can I give you my answer by tomorrow?" This allows her to assess her schedule, priorities, and desire to attend, ultimately leading to a response that aligns with her needs.

- **Fear of Rejection:** The pressure to be liked and accepted can make women hesitant to make choices that might be perceived negatively by others, leading to indecision.

- **Fear of Missing Out (FOMO): this** can be a powerful emotion. However, the 'I Need Time to Think' tactic allows you to gather information and weigh the potential benefits against your priorities. This can help you make a confident decision that aligns with your goals, even if it means missing out on something else."

- **Lack of Confidence:** Societal messages about gender roles between men and women can create self-doubt, making women question their judgment and abilities to make the "right" decision.

From Hesitant to Super Hero: "I Need Time to Think" to Shine

Scenario: Sarah is in a meeting at work where a complex technical decision needs to be made. She has a good idea about the best course of action but hesitates to speak up because she worries she might be wrong and doesn't want to appear incompetent.

1. **1. Gather Information & Clarify Doubts:** Sarah can use the "I Need Time to Think" tactic to gain confidence. She could say, "This is a great point. I have some thoughts on the best approach. I'd like to take a moment to gather some additional information (data, past experiences) to ensure I'm presenting the most well-rounded solution."

2. Formulate her Recommendation: While reflecting, Sarah can:

- Review relevant data and past projects.
- Consider potential risks and benefits of different options.
- Formulate a clear and concise recommendation based on her analysis.

3. Confident Communication: When Sarah rejoins the discussion, she can speak with increased confidence. She can share her well-researched recommendation, highlighting the data and reasoning behind it. By taking the time to think, she avoids blurting out an under-developed idea and demonstrates a thoughtful approach.

Taking time allows Sarah to overcome her initial self-doubt and present a well-supported recommendation, positioning her as a valuable contributor. This can boost her confidence in future situations.

The "I Need Time to Think" tactic can be a powerful tool for buyers as well. It allows you to make informed decisions that align with your needs and budget, avoiding the buyer's remorse that often follows rushed purchases. However, saying no to a salesperson can be a challenge. Here, we explore some common hurdles buyers face:

Building Confidence in Your Decision: A Savvy Shopper Prioritizing Value

Interviewer: Hi Amelia, thanks for joining me today. Can you tell us about a time when you used the "I Need Time to Think" tactic to avoid a potentially bad purchase?

Amelia: Absolutely! I'd been eyeing a new designer bag for weeks. It was beautiful, trendy, and everything my friends were raving about. I saw it on sale at a high-end department store and felt a surge of excitement.

Interviewer: Sounds like a dream come true! What made you hesitate before buying it?

Amelia: The price tag. While it was on sale, it was still a significant investment. It gnawed at me – Was this a practical purchase? Did it fit my long-term style? Honestly, I didn't want to make a decision based solely on the thrill of the sale.

Interviewer: How did you use the "I Need Time to Think" tactic in this situation?

Amelia: I politely thanked the salesperson and explained that I loved the bag but wanted time to think about it overnight. I also mentioned I was open to exploring other styles in my budget.

Interviewer: Did the salesperson resist the delay?

Amelia: A bit. They tried to close the sale with additional discounts and limited-time offers. But I remained firm. I explained that a thoughtful purchase would make me happier in the long run.

Interviewer: Did taking the time to think ultimately lead to a better outcome?

Amelia: Absolutely! After sleeping on it, I realized the bag was more of a trend piece that wouldn't fit my wardrobe for long. Instead, I used the money saved to invest in a timeless, high-quality leather tote that I knew I'd use for years to come.

Interviewer: Sounds like a wise decision. Do you have any advice for other shoppers facing similar situations?

Amelia: Definitely! Here are a few tips:

- **Don't be pressured by sales tactics.** High-pressure tactics are used to create a sense of urgency and cloud your judgment. It's okay to walk away and come back later.

- **Consider your needs and budget.** Don't get swayed by trends or impulse buys. Ask yourself if the item aligns with your personal style and long-term needs.

- **Shop around and compare prices.** Don't assume the first offer is the best. Research other retailers and compare prices before making a purchase.

- **Sleep on it.** Give yourself some time to cool down and analyze the purchase objectively. Will you still love it tomorrow? Does it fit your budget?

Interviewer: Thank you, Amelia, for sharing your experience. Your story highlights the importance of taking time to make informed decisions as a shopper, prioritizing value and practicality over impulsive purchases when facing a salesperson's pressure tactics and the potential for buyer's remorse. By requesting time to think, you empower yourself to resist the urge for an impulsive purchase and confidently purchase something else with long-term value.

By understanding the root causes and taking steps to empower yourself, you can become a brilliant and resilient decision-maker, shattering the stereotype once and for all.

Sometimes, the situation might not require a full-blown conversation or negotiation. There are times when a polite but firm decline is necessary. While simply saying "no" can work, the "I Need Time to Think" tactic, opens a space for conversation and a solution that works for everyone. This pause allows them to gather information, understand each other's concerns, and ultimately reach a mutually beneficial agreement. In Chapter 8 we explore a more nuanced approach: The Art of the Gracious Decline: "I Can't Commit to This as I Have Other Priorities."

Chapter 8: The Art Of "I Can't Commit To This As I Have Other Priorities At The Moment" Strategy: Teamwork Through Delegation

"We need to free ourselves up to be more creative. And the only way to do that is to delegate." - Arianna Huffington, Co-founder of The Huffington Post

*****

The Power of "We": How Saying "I Can't Commit" Saved My Sanity (and My Marriage)

Jessica stared at the ever-growing list on the refrigerator door. Dinner party for ten? Check. Book club meeting? Check. Soccer practice carpool for the entire week? Check, check, check. A familiar knot of tension tightened in her shoulders. "Just another day in the life of Supermom," she muttered under her breath.

"Hey honey," he said, pecking her on the cheek. "Busy night?"

"Just finalizing things for the weekend," Jessica replied tightly, forcing a smile.

David scanned the list. "Wow, that's a lot. You sure you can handle it all?"

"Handle it?" Jessica repeated, her smile faltering. "David, this isn't just 'handling it.' This is grocery shopping, menu planning, decorating, prepping ten portions of food, not to mention cleaning the house before everyone arrives."

David's smile softened. "Whoa, okay, I see your point. What can I do to help?"

Jessica hesitated. Saying no outright felt wrong, but the thought of adding more tasks to her already overflowing plate was overwhelming. Then, she remembered the "I can't commit" strategy.

Taking a deep breath, she said, "Honey," Jessica said, channeling her inner Wonder Woman, "I can't save the world *and* conquer this mountain of laundry. Maybe we can call in a Justice League of family members to help?"

A flicker of surprise crossed David's face, and then understanding dawned. "So, what do you need from me?"

"Well," Jessica began, "maybe you could handle the grocery shopping this week? We could look at the menu together and delegate some prep tasks. And maybe the kids can help with some simple cleaning chores before the party?"

David readily agreed. "Absolutely! Let's split the list, and I can take the kids to the park on Saturday afternoon to give you some prep time."

Relief washed over Jessica. By simply stating her limitations and collaborating with David, she'd not only lightened her load but also created a more balanced partnership.

The weekend arrived, and the house buzzed with activity. David expertly navigated the grocery store, the kids proudly helped dust the living room shelves, and Jessica, with her stress levels under control, whipped up a delicious meal. The party was a success, filled with laughter and good company.

Later that night, nestled on the couch with David, Jessica felt a newfound appreciation for the "I can't commit" strategy. It wasn't about saying no to her family, but about saying yes to a more balanced and supportive way of running their household. They had tackled the challenge together, and in the process, strengthened their bond as a team.

*****

Empowering Your Family: How Delegation Creates a Connected and Thriving Household

Imagine your family as a beautiful symphony orchestra. Each member represents a different instrument, with unique skills and strengths. The conductor (you) has the responsibility to create a harmonious performance.

Trying to do everything yourself is like the conductor trying to play every instrument alone. The result? A cacophony of noise, frustration, and missed potential.

Delegation is like assigning the right instruments to the right musicians. When a young child is given the triangle, they learn rhythm and contribute their part. A teenager might be entrusted with a recorder, practicing melody and following instructions. Parents, with their experience, can handle the more complex instruments like the violin or cello.

Clear communication is the sheet music. It ensures everyone understands their part and plays in sync. The "why" behind a task becomes the melody, motivating each member to contribute. When instructions are clear, the music flows smoothly.

- **Empowers Others:** Delegation shows trust in family members, allowing them to develop new skills and a sense of ownership over tasks. This builds confidence and fosters a sense of accomplishment.

- **Fosters Teamwork:** When everyone contributes, it creates a sense of shared responsibility and teamwork. Family members learn to collaborate, communicate effectively, and work towards a common goal.

- **Teaches Valuable Life Skills:** Delegation allows children (and even some adults!) to practice important skills like time management, organization, problem-solving, and hand-eye co-ordination from folding laundry and math skills like fractions when cooking. The value of these life skills learned at home are lasting and benefit them in all areas of life.

● **Strengthens Bonds:** Working together on shared tasks can create a sense of unity and connection within a family. It allows for bonding experiences and fosters a sense of interdependence, each one is their own individual but can depend on others and can be depended upon in a mutual given and receive.

● **Improves Efficiency:** By delegating tasks to those who are most skilled or have the most time, families can achieve more in less time. This frees up time for everyone to relax, pursue hobbies, or spend quality time together.

Speak Clearly, Delegate Smoothly: Communication Tips for a Thriving Family Team

Clear communication is the cornerstone of successful delegation. When everyone understands their role and the "why" behind a task, it sets the stage for smooth execution and a sense of ownership. Here's how to use communication to empower your family members and identify tasks ripe for delegation:

- **Break Down the Task:** Explain the task in simple, achievable steps. For younger children, demonstrate the steps if necessary.

- **Set Clear Expectations:** Outline the desired outcome, including deadlines and quality standards. Hold up a neatly folded t-shirt as an example when delegating laundry, or show your teenager a recipe for a dish they'll be helping prepare.

- **Match Skills and Time:** Consider the age and skill level of the family member you're delegating to. Younger children can handle simpler tasks like sorting socks or setting the table, while teenagers might be entrusted with more complex chores like mowing the lawn (with proper training) or helping with meal planning.

- **Foster Ownership:** Explain why this task is important for the smooth running of the household. Perhaps mention how clean laundry makes everyone feel good, or how a delicious meal brings the family together.

- **Open Communication is Key:** Encourage questions and clarification. Let family members know you're available for support throughout the process.

By following these communication tips, you can transform seemingly mundane chores into opportunities for learning, teamwork, and shared responsibility.

"Alright, team meeting!" Sarah called out, gathering her two teenagers around. "Laundry duty is on deck, but before we dive in, let's make a battle plan. Think of it like a superhero training session. You two are Laundry Lad and Sock Slayer, and I'm your wise (slightly sleep-deprived) mentor."

Following her own advice, Sarah started by breaking down the task. "First, we need to sort the clothes by color. Lights go here, darks over there." She pointed to designated hampers.

Next came defining expectations. "Success means everything gets clean and folded, ready to be put away." Sarah held up a neatly folded t-shirt as an example.

Knowing her teens' busy schedules, Sarah set a realistic deadline. "We can aim to finish by dinnertime, but if anyone needs more time, just let me know."

Creating a safe space for questions was key. "Don't hesitate to ask if anything is unclear," she emphasized. "Folding fitted sheets can be tricky, so I'm happy to help!"

Finally, Sarah offered support. "Remember, we're a team in this," she said with a smile. "Let's put on some music and make laundry day fun!"

*****

By implementing these simple communication tips, Sarah transformed a potentially stressful chore into a collaborative family activity. By taking the time to communicate clearly when you delegate tasks, you'll be setting everyone up for success. This leads to a more efficient and harmonious family environment, where everyone feels empowered to contribute.

Boost Your Family's Superpowers: Unleash Efficiency and Teamwork Through Delegation

Delegation isn't just about offloading chores! It's a strategic way to empower others and build a more efficient family unit. However, not every task is a good candidate for delegation. Here are some tips to help you identify tasks that can be delegated effectively:

Characteristics of Delegatable Tasks:

- **Skill Level:** Is the task appropriate for the skills and age of the person you're delegating to? Consider offering scaled-down versions of complex tasks for younger children.

- **Time Commitment:** Is the task manageable within the person's existing schedule? Don't overload someone who already has a lot on their plate.

- **Clear Instructions:** Can the task be clearly explained with specific steps and an achievable outcome? The easier it is to understand, the more likely it will be completed successfully.

- **Learning Opportunity:** Does the task offer a chance for the person to develop new skills or take on more responsibility? Look for opportunities for growth.

- **Safety Considerations:** Is the task safe for the person to complete? Consider age and maturity level when delegating tasks that involve potential hazards.

Examples of Delegatable Tasks:

- **Age-Appropriate Chores:** Matching socks, setting the table, unloading groceries, taking out the trash – these are all great options for younger children.

- **Yard Work:** Raking leaves, weeding gardens, mowing the lawn (with proper training and safety precautions) – older children can contribute significantly to outdoor chores.

- **Simple Errands:** Picking up dry cleaning, running to the store for a forgotten ingredient – these can be delegated to teenagers or responsible older children.

- **Research and Planning:** Teens can help research family vacation ideas, plan a birthday party, or even create a grocery list.

Remember: Delegation is a learning process for everyone involved. Be patient and offer support as the person becomes familiar with their new responsibilities. Celebrate their successes, and use feedback to adjust expectations and communication styles for future tasks. By delegating effectively, you'll empower your family members, build a stronger team, and free up valuable time for everyone to enjoy!

The Multiplier Effect: A Confident And Resilient Culture At Work

Knowing when to involve a colleague or supervisor is a crucial skill in the workplace. It demonstrates initiative, collaboration, and a commitment to quality work. Here are some key situations when involving others is the right call:

- **Workload Overload:** Your plate is overflowing, and meeting deadlines feels impossible. Don't be a silent martyr! Involve your supervisor to discuss workload adjustments or delegation opportunities.

- **Lack of Expertise:** The task requires specialized knowledge you don't possess. Involving a colleague with relevant expertise ensures the project is completed effectively and efficiently.

- **Need for Feedback or Brainstorming:** Sometimes a fresh perspective is invaluable. Involving colleagues can spark new ideas, identify potential pitfalls, and improve the overall quality of your work.

- **Ethical Dilemmas:** You encounter a situation that raises ethical concerns. Don't navigate this alone. Involving your supervisor ensures transparency and protects you and the company or clients from potential consequences.

- **Decision-Making Impasse:** You're stuck between two options and can't make a clear decision. Involving your supervisor or colleagues can provide valuable insights and lead to a more informed decision.

By involving others strategically, you not only share the workload and tap into valuable expertise, but you also foster collaboration, build trust with colleagues, and demonstrate strong problem-solving skills.

Empowering Others and Streamlining Workflows

Delegation isn't just about offloading tasks. It's about strategically assigning work to others, allowing them to develop new skills and take ownership.

- **Identify Tasks:** Choose tasks appropriate for the person's skill level and workload and tell them why their skills are being chosen for this task.

- **Clear Instructions:** Provide clear and concise instructions, outlining expectations and deadlines.

- **Set Up for Success:** Offer support and resources to ensure the person has everything they need to complete the task effectively.

- **Empowerment and Ownership:** Encourage the person to ask questions and make decisions within a defined scope.

- **Provide Feedback:** Offer constructive feedback to help them grow and improve.

The "I can't commit to this as I have other priorities at the moment" strategy can be a valuable tool for managing your workload at work, however, it is important to use it tactfully and professionally. Here's an example:

Scenario: You're in a team meeting where your manager assigns a new project with a tight deadline. You already have several high-priority tasks on your plate, and taking on this new project could lead to feeling overwhelmed or missed deadlines on your existing commitments.

Here's how to use the strategy effectively:

1. Acknowledge the Request:

"Thanks for assigning this project, [Manager's name]. It sounds interesting."

2. Express Your Current Workload:

"However, I'm currently swamped with [briefly mention your existing priorities]. Taking on this new project with the current deadline might impact my ability to deliver high-quality work on everything."

3. Offer Solutions:

"Would it be possible to [suggest alternative solutions, such as extending the deadline, delegating some tasks, or prioritizing with your manager]? I'm confident I can contribute effectively to this project within those parameters."

4. Show Willingness:

"Regardless, I'm happy to discuss this further and find a way to move forward that works for everyone."

By using this strategy effectively, you can manage your workload and ensure you're delivering the best possible results on all your projects.

Benefits of Delegation:

- Increased productivity for everyone, first you get good then you get fast.

- Development of new skills in team members

- Improved team morale and collaboration

- Free up your time to focus on higher-level tasks

Benefits of Effective Communication:

- Reduced misunderstandings and errors
- Increased trust and collaboration
- Improved problem-solving and decision-making
- Stronger working relationships
- More efficient use of time and resources

Consider all the people this kind of assertiveness ripples out to and the potential for positive benefits in their lives. What happens when "no" is the only answer that comes to mind in the moment? Delegation is a powerful tool, but there will be times when your family's A-Team is already stretched thin. That's where the art of offering alternatives becomes crucial.

Instead of shutting down requests completely, we can explore creative solutions that work for everyone. Just because you can't say "yes" right now, doesn't mean you can't find a way to make it happen "later" or in a different way.

In Chapter 9: Offering Alternatives: "Now Is Not A Good Time" Strategy, a temporary no now but leaving the door open to negotiate a future time.

Chapter 9: The Art Of "Now Is Not A Good Time" Strategy: Pillars of Self-Care

"We need women who are not afraid to be vulnerable. We need women who are not afraid to be powerful. We need women who are not afraid to be both." - Audre Lorde, Poet, Activist

*****

From Tears to Triumph: A Woman's Journey to Radiant Resilience

Amelia clutched the crumpled tissue in her hand, tears threatening to spill again. Dr. Wright's office, usually a haven of serenity, felt suffocating. Across from her, Dr. Wright's brow furrowed with concern.

"Amelia," Dr. Wright said gently, "your test results are in, and they paint a concerning picture."

Amelia's heart hammered against her ribs. "What is it, Dr. Wright?"

"The diagnosis is overwhelm," Dr. Wright said carefully. "Your body is showing signs of chronic stress – high blood pressure, fatigue, even the recent panic attack."

Amelia's breath hitched. Overwhelm? It felt like a foreign word, yet it described her life perfectly. She could no longer deny the effects of the relentless demands of her CEO position, the never-ending to-do list at home, or the constant feeling of being stretched thin that was taking a toll on her well-being. Hearing the words from Dr. Wright and knowing it was the truth, Amelia felt frustration as she held back a flood of tears that were about to flow.

"But... how can overwhelm be a medical condition?" Amelia whispered, voice thick with emotion.

"Think of it like this, Amelia," Dr. Wright said, leaning forward. "Our bodies are designed to handle stress in short bursts. But when that stress becomes chronic, relentless – like yours has – it starts to take a toll on your physical and mental well-being."

Shame washed over Amelia. "I've been pushing myself too hard, haven't I?"

Dr. Wright offered a sympathetic smile. "Many women do, Amelia. We juggle so much, often neglecting our own needs."

A tear escaped, tracing a glistening path down Amelia's cheek. "But what do I do? I can't just... stop everything."

"No, of course not," Dr. Wright assured her. "But you can start saying no more often. Start prioritizing your well-being. Think of it as preventative medicine."

Intrigued, Amelia wiped her tears. "Preventative medicine? How?"

Dr. Wright explained the concept of "now is not a good time" as a powerful tool. She spoke about setting boundaries, both at work and at home. Amelia listened intently, a flicker of hope igniting within her.

"It's not about selfishness, Amelia," Dr. Wright emphasized. "It's about self-preservation. You can't pour from an empty cup. By taking care of yourself, you'll be better equipped to handle everything life throws your way."

Amelia took a deep breath, feeling a weight begin to lift. This wasn't a magic solution, but it was a lifeline. Dr. Wright's guidance, Amelia knew she could reclaim her health and rediscover the vibrant woman buried beneath the overwhelm.

"Thank you, Dr. Wright," Amelia said, a newfound determination in her voice. "For the diagnosis, and the hope."

Dr. Wright smiled warmly. "The journey to radiant resilience starts now with a self-care plan, Amelia. And remember, you're not alone."

*****

The Pillars of Self-Care: Nourishing Your Physical, Mental, Emotional, and Spiritual Needs

1. A self-care plan is a personalized roadmap, a proactive approach to prioritizing your physical, mental, and emotional well-being. Here's a breakdown of its key elements: **1. Identify Your Needs:**

● **Physical:** This includes sleep hygiene, a balanced diet, and regular exercise.

● **Mental:** This encompasses activities that stimulate your mind and promote relaxation, like reading, meditation, or pursuing hobbies.

● **Emotional:** This focuses on strategies to manage stress, build healthy relationships, and nurture your emotional well-being, this could be engaging in art or listening to your favorite music, who are the people/relationships that support and uplift you?

● **Spiritual:** This involves connecting with your values, finding purpose, or engaging in practices that nourish your spirit and with life force energy. This doesn't necessarily mean religion, it could be as simple as bird watching, taking a walk in nature, or sitting by the lake or river, whatever uplifts you and reminds you that you are a part of something greater. This will inspire a sense of awe and wonder at the vastness of the world and the possibilities for all that is.

2. Remember your "why": Remind yourself often why protecting your time and energy matters.

● Visualize the benefits – a happier you, a more fulfilling life.

● Clearly define what you want your desired end result to be with your self-care for managing stress and negative emotions.

● Ensure your health goals align with your core values.

● **3. Schedule self-care activities:** Delegate time in your calendar for activities that nourish your well-being.

● **4. Establish boundaries:** Learn to say "no" and prioritize your needs, focusing on the emotion of the end result you want. What will having this give you that you think you don't already have?

● **5. Build a support system:** Schedule time in your agenda to surround yourself with positive people who encourage and support your self-care journey.

● **6. Practice self-compassion:** Would you expect a friend to feel guilty about saying no? Treat yourself with the same kindness and understanding.

● **7. Celebrate achievements:** Acknowledge yourself for sticking to your self-care plan.

The Lies We Believe: Why Guilt is Holding You Back

Guilt, in this context, is an emotional response triggered by the perception that you have done something wrong or fallen short of your expectations, or those of others. It can manifest in various ways, including:

- **Self-blame:** Feeling responsible for a negative outcome, even if the situation wasn't entirely your fault.

- **Regret:** Wishing you had acted differently in a past situation.

- **Anxiety:** Worrying about the consequences of your actions or the potential disappointment you may cause others.

- **Shame:** Feeling a deep sense of unworthiness or inadequacy due to your perceived wrongdoing.

- **Identify the source:** The guilt cycle focuses on the societal pressure women often face to prioritize the needs of others over their own. Saying "no" can trigger guilt because it challenges this expectation and can lead to the fear of being seen as selfish or inconsiderate.

- **Fear of failure:** Saying "no" might feel like admitting defeat or inability to handle everything. This can be especially prevalent in high-achieving women who tie their value to their productivity.

- **Fear of letting people down:** We want to be seen as reliable and dependable. Saying "no" can create anxiety about disappointing others or damaging relationships.

- **Fear of missing out (FOMO):** There's a constant pressure to be present at all events and involved in every opportunity. Saying "no" can trigger the fear of missing out on something important or losing opportunities.

● **Fear of judgment:** Our society often praises women who sacrifice and "do it all." Saying "no" can lead to the fear of being judged as lazy, uncommitted, or not dedicated enough.

● **Belief in the "superwoman" myth:** Many women internalize the belief that they have the capacity to handle everything perfectly and if they do "they are worthy or enough".

● **Internalized gender roles:** Traditional gender roles often place the burden of caregiving and emotional labor on women. Saying "no" can feel like neglecting your responsibilities or failing if you do not prioritize the needs of others.

These fears and beliefs can all contribute to the guilt cycle. The good news is that with a little self-awareness, we can challenge these unconscious programs and flip them all to become your greatest Superpower and personal ally. A belief is only an idea that we have accepted as truth, usually before we had any ability to determine if the source of the information was accurate or not.

"No" Means Opportunity: Reframing Your Mindset for Graceful Declines

● **Shift the script:** Instead of "no," think of it as "not right now." This allows for flexibility and other possibilities, it avoids feeling like a complete shutdown.

● **Focus on the positive:** Saying "no" allows you to say "yes" to something more important, whether it's self-care, time with loved ones, or focusing on a critical task. One possible alternative is that the person making the request may find someone else who is available to meet their need, maybe there is a change in their schedule that freed up time and they can now do it themselves.

"Now is not a good time" becomes a Bridge for Mutual Success

Instead of a dead end, "now is not a good time" unlocks a door to positive opportunities. It opens the door for a more suitable time to collaborate, allows you to suggest a better fit for the task, or creates space for alternative solutions. It's not a roadblock, but a pathway towards a win-win situation.

"Now is not a good time" becomes a "Life Management Superhero" phrase.

Imagine yourself juggling a circus act of responsibilities. Saying "Now is not a good time" allows you to step back, assess the experience, and prioritize the tasks you can handle effectively. You become a "Time Management Superhero," ensuring everything gets done, but on your terms, at your pace, and with a clear focus. Remember: The outcome of daily experiences does not define you as a whole human being. **You** are so much more than the outcome of a meeting, the laundry pile, or missing a dinner invite.

Artful Dodge Manifesto: Your Personal Boundary Blueprint

The Artful Dodge Manifesto is your statement outlining your boundaries and preferred communication methods. It's your superpower for politely declining requests while fostering respect and clarity.

Here's a template to guide you in crafting your manifesto:

My Artful Dodge Manifesto

My Core Values:

- [Value 1] (e.g., work-life balance, health, creativity)
- [Value 2] (e.g., family time, personal growth, quality over quantity)

To protect my time and energy, I prefer communication via:

- [Preferred method 1] (e.g., email) during [available hours] (e.g., weekdays between 9 AM and 5 PM)

- [Preferred method 2] (e.g., text message) for urgent matters only

If something falls outside my current availability, I might respond with "now is not a good time" but will offer alternative solutions whenever possible.

Thank you for respecting my boundaries!

Example Artful Dodge Manifesto:

- **My Core Values:** Work-life balance and mental well-being.

- To protect my time and energy, I prefer communication via Email during weekdays between 9 AM and 5 PM. I check voicemail and text messages periodically throughout the day but prioritize responding to emails.

- If something falls outside my current availability, I might respond with "now is not a good time" but will offer alternative solutions whenever possible. For example, I could suggest a specific time for a call or meeting, or offer to address the request in a future email.

● Thank you for respecting my boundaries!

Remember, this is just a template. Feel free to personalize it to reflect your unique needs and preferences.

Scenario 1: The Social Butterfly

You: Introverted writer who cherishes quiet time for creative work.

Situation: A friend invites you to a weekend-long music festival known for its loud crowds and constant activity.

Artful Dodge: "That sounds like a lot of fun, but big crowds aren't really my scene. I have a writing deadline this month and need some focused quiet time. Maybe we can grab coffee next week and catch up then?"

Explanation: You acknowledge the appeal of the invitation while honoring your need for introverted peace and quiet. You offer an alternative to maintain the social connection.

Scenario 2: The Family Obligation

You: An Adult child with a demanding job who prioritizes spending quality time with your partner.

Situation: Your parents frequently call on you for last-minute errands or chores, often interrupting your date nights.

Artful Dodge: "I appreciate you thinking of me, but [partner's name] and I have planned a special dinner tonight. Maybe I can swing by on [alternative day] to help with those errands?"

Explanation: You express gratitude for the request while emphasizing your pre-existing commitment. You suggest an alternative solution to maintain a helpful relationship with your parents.

Scenario 3: The Workaholic Colleague

You: Value work-life balance and setting boundaries with colleagues.

Situation: A colleague frequently emails you work requests late at night or on weekends, disrupting your personal time.

Artful Dodge: "Thanks for sending this over! Mondays are a great time for me to catch up on emails. In the meantime, enjoy your well-deserved weekend!"

Explanation: You set a clear boundary by establishing your preferred communication timeframe. You subtly remind them to respect your personal time.

By crafting your Artful Dodge Manifesto, you take charge of your communication and empower yourself to say "no" with grace and clarity. Remember, setting boundaries isn't selfish; it's essential for creating a healthy life that thrives. Now you can reclaim your time, radiate resilience, and satisfy your life on your terms!

Scenario 4: The Weekend Warrior

You: Aspiring marathon runner who prioritizes physical fitness for upcoming races.

Situation: A colleague invites you to join them for after-work drinks every Friday, a tradition they cherish.

Artful Dodge: "That sounds fun, but Fridays are dedicated to my long training runs for my upcoming marathon! I wouldn't want to miss a key workout. Maybe we could grab coffee or lunch sometime next week to celebrate your weekend?"

Explanation: You acknowledge the appeal of their offer while emphasizing your commitment to training. You suggest an alternative activity to maintain the social connection and celebrate their weekend plans. This emphasizes respect for their tradition while prioritizing your own goals.

The Power of A Graceful Decline

You've mastered the art of "now is not a good time" and crafted your Artful Dodge Manifesto. Now what? What happens when even the most tempting alternative just doesn't fit? This is where the true power of graceful decline shines.

Respecting Your Boundaries

Saying no to an alternative isn't about being difficult to get along with; it's about honoring your boundaries. You've identified your priorities and created your Artful Dodge Manifesto. This is your chance to put it into practice, protecting your precious time and energy.

Avoiding Overcommitment

Remember, saying yes to an alternative, even with good intentions, can lead to over-commitment and ultimately cause burnout. Saying no can feel counter-intuitive, but in the long run, it allows you to focus on what truly matters without feeling overwhelmed.

Prioritizing Self-Care

Sometimes, the best "alternative" is simply saying no and prioritizing self-care. It allows you to recharge and come-back stronger for the things that truly matter. Don't feel guilty about taking care of yourself!

Beyond "No": The Art of Saying No with Grace and Strength

So, how do you say no to alternatives with grace and clarity? Here are some key strategies:

- **Clarity and Honesty:** Be clear and upfront about your limitations. "Thank you for suggesting [alternative], but unfortunately, that doesn't work for me either."

- **Gratitude and Appreciation:** Express your appreciation for the offer and their understanding. "I truly appreciate you trying to find a solution."

- **Future Availability (Optional):** If appropriate, offer another time when you will be available to help. "Perhaps we can revisit this in [timeframe]."

- **Sticking to Your Guns:** It's perfectly okay to repeat your no. Don't feel pressured to justify your decision. A simple "No, thank you" is sufficient.

Saying no to alternatives isn't rude; it's self-respectful. It's a demonstration of strength and self-awareness, and the foundation for a radiant and resilient life. By mastering the art of graceful decline, you cultivate a life where your "no" means no, and your time and energy are used for the things that truly matter.

You mastered the art of saying "no," set personal boundaries on time, and the best methods of communication that work for you but there are some situations where a request is made that don't align with you. Chapter 10: "I'm Not The Best Person To Help With This" explores navigating requests outside your expertise. Join us as we delve into the art of graceful decline and ensuring clear communication.

Chapter 10: The Art Of "I'm Not The Best Person To Help With This" Strategy: Empowering Others

"I've learned that people will forget what you said, people will forget what you did, but people will never forget how you made them feel." - Maya Angelou, Poet, Activist

*****

No Doesn't Dim Your Light, It Sparks Theirs: The Magic of Saying No

Kinslee nervously adjusted the strap of her messenger bag, the worn leather cool against her clammy hand. Across the cafe table sat her friend, Maise, a whirlwind of energy and infectious enthusiasm.

"So, Kinslee," Maisie began, her eyes sparkling, "I'm starting this amazing new program at the community center – after-school coding for underprivileged girls! And I thought, you being a total tech wiz, would be perfect to help me get it off the ground!"

Kinslee's stomach lurched. Her love for Maisie warred with the familiar knot of guilt that tightened in her chest whenever presented with a new request. She took a deep breath, summoning the lessons from her well-worn copy of "Radiant Resilience."

"Maisie, that sounds incredible!" she said, genuinely excited for her friend. "And I truly admire you embracing this initiative. Unfortunately, with the launch of my app next month, my schedule is slammed." This was the "Shiny Object Syndrome" Kinslee had been warned about. Maisie's project, while inspiring, would stretch her already thin resources.

"Oh, I completely understand," Maisie said, her smile faltering slightly. "I know you're super busy with the app."

Kinslee saw an opening for the "Empowerment through Delegation" strategy. "But I know someone who might be a great fit! Remember Elaine from our coding group last year? She's brilliant and passionate about getting young girls interested in tech."

Maisie's smile returned, brighter this time. "Oh my gosh, that's perfect! I completely forgot about Elaine. Thank you so much, Kinslee!"

Relief washed over Kinslee, replaced by a warm sense of accomplishment. Saying "no" had not dimmed Maisie's enthusiasm; it had opened doors for Elaine, allowing her friend to fulfill her vision while Kinslee focused on her mission.

Later that night, nestled under her favorite blanket with her laptop open, Kinslee started brainstorming marketing strategies for her app. A notification popped up – an email from Elaine, thanking her for the connection and expressing her excitement about the community center program. A genuine smile bloomed on Kinslee's face. This, she thought, was radiance redefined – the ability to say "no" with grace while letting others shine and showcase a collaborative spirit.

*****

Dodging the Over-commitment Octopus: "I'm Not the Best Person for This, But..."

Have you ever felt overwhelmed by requests on your time? The over-commitment Octopus, with its eight suction-cupped arms, loves attaching itself to busy achievers. It whispers promises of endless opportunities, but ultimately leaves you feeling stretched thin and overwhelmed.

The "Rescuer on Repeat" in Action

- **The Perpetual "Yes Woman":** You constantly get pulled into helping colleagues with their overflowing to-do lists, even when it stretches your resources thin. This can leave you feeling drained and resentful.

- **The Social Media Savior:** A friend pleads with you to completely revamp their social media presence while managing your own accounts. Saying "yes" can lead to burnout and neglecting your own projects.

- **The Committee Conundrum:** You feel pressured to join every committee at work, neglecting your personal goals and becoming overwhelmed by the additional workload.

- **The "Fear of Missing Out"** You worry that saying "no" means missing out on potential growth or connections. Example: An acquaintance invites you to speak at a conference outside your expertise, but you fear declining will limit your networking opportunities.

Saying no can be hard. But it's essential. Here's how to use the "I'm Not the Best Person for This" strategy:

Step 1: Acknowledge and Appreciate: Let the requester know you appreciate their offer or invitation. "Thank you so much for thinking of me for [opportunity]."

Step 2: Explain Why You're Not the Best Fit: Use the phrase "I'm not the best person for this" followed by a clear, concise reason.

- **Skills Gap:** "Unfortunately, I don't have the expertise in [area] that this project requires."

- **Time Constraints:** "My schedule is full right now."

- **Values Mismatch:** "While this cause is important, it doesn't align with my current focus on [your area]."

- **Language Barrier.** "I'd love to give this presentation but my translation skills to speak to this audience aren't quite what they need to be yet."

Step 3: Offer an Alternative (Optional) [current project] right now." This step elevates your "no" from a dead-end to a bridge of potential.

- **Empowerment through Delegation:** "But I know someone who might be perfect! [Name someone] is a whiz at [relevant skill]."

- **Suggest a Resource:** "Perhaps I can offer some resources that might be helpful. [Website/book suggestion]."

Remember:

- Be honest and upfront about your limitations.

- Use a positive and helpful tone.

- By offering alternatives, you are still demonstrating support for the requester's goals even if you can't directly contribute.

Beyond the Glimmer: Discerning True Opportunities from Distractions

Have you ever fallen prey to the "Shiny Object Syndrome"? You know the feeling – a dazzling opportunity arises, followed by another, each promising a path to success. The temptation to chase them all is strong, but here's the secret most never tell you: focus fuels brilliance.

Imagine yourself at the helm of a mighty ship, navigating towards a specific destination. Every new "shiny object" – a tempting project, an exciting collaboration – acts like a siren song, luring you off course. Chasing each one may seem productive, but in reality, it creates a multitasking mirage. You spread yourself thin, your efforts diluted, reaching none of your destinations with true impact.

Here's the Radiantly Real truth: laser focus is the key to unleashing your inner powerhouse. By channelling your energy towards a clear passion and core value, you hone your skills, deepen your expertise, and ultimately, shine brighter.

So, the next time a captivating opportunity catches your eye, pause.Ask yourself: "Does this truly align with my long-term vision? Will it propel me towards my desired end result, or distract me from the journey?" The pressure to say yes can feel like a tidal wave, threatening to drown your time and energy. A strategic "no" today may feel like a missed chance, but in reality, it's a powerful step towards a future overflowing with radiant success.

Example of a Shiny Object (For Creatives):

Let's say you are a blossoming graphic designer, steadily building a portfolio of sleek and impactful logos. You land a coveted client who wants you to design their logo but also throws in the additional tasks of revamping their entire website and creating a social media branding strategy. While this project sounds extensive and lucrative, it pulls you away from your core strength – logo design – and forces you to potentially spread yourself thin across unfamiliar territory. This shiny object, while a seemingly grand opportunity, could dilute the quality of your logo work and delay your progress toward establishing yourself as a top logo designer.

Example of a Shiny Object:(For Consultants)

Let's say you're a brilliant financial advisor, diligently building a reputation for helping clients achieve their long-term investment goals. Suddenly, a colleague approaches you with the opportunity to co-host a financial podcast. While the podcast could be a fantastic way to reach a wider audience, it requires a significant time commitment and a shift in focus from one-on-one client consultations to broader market commentary. This shiny object, while potentially beneficial, could distract you from your core expertise and slow your progress toward establishing yourself as a top financial advisor.

Example of a Shiny Object (For Management):

Imagine you're a rising star manager, leading a team towards consistently exceeding sales quotas. You're known for your talent in developing your team members' strengths and fostering a collaborative environment. Suddenly, your boss proposes you take on a new leadership role overseeing a different department, known for its operational inefficiencies. While this opportunity could lead to a significant promotion, it requires a major shift in focus, pulling you away from your core strength – team development – and potentially jeopardizing the continued success of your current team. This shiny object, while a seemingly prestigious step up, could dilute your impact and delay your progress while establishing yourself as a top manager known for empowering high-performing teams.

Don't Force the Fit: Chasing Your Ideal Puzzle Picture (and Saying No to the Rest)

The "Mismatched Puzzle Piece" describes situations where a seemingly perfect opportunity doesn't align with your skills, experience, or goals. Like a puzzle piece with the wrong shape, forcing yourself into these projects leads to frustration and wasted effort.

The "Skills Gap": The request requires expertise you don't possess.

- Example: A men's magazine asks you to write an article about navigating the stock market, a topic outside your financial writing niche.

- "Thank you for thinking of me! While I'm passionate about personal finance, my expertise lies in [your specific niche, e.g., budgeting for families]. I would be happy to connect you with some fantastic financial writers specializing in stock market analysis."

The "Time Zone Tango": Logistical hurdles like time zone differences or travel constraints impede your ability to deliver effectively.

- Example: An international organization invites you to participate in a weekly online forum, but the time commitment clashes with your writing sessions.

- "I'm so grateful for the invitation to join your forum. However, due to the time zone difference and my current writing deadlines, I wouldn't be able to participate as actively as I'd like. Perhaps you could consider pre-recording some of my insights, or I might be able to contribute a guest article on [relevant topic]."

The "Values Mismatch": The project or cause conflicts with your core values or purpose.

- Example: A company known for unethical practices asks you to endorse their product, contradicting your commitment to social responsibility.

- "Thank you for reaching out. While I admire your company's [positive aspect, e.g., innovation], I'm very selective about the products I endorse because of my strong commitment to [your core value, e.g., sustainability]. I wish you all the best in your endeavors."

Beyond the Ego: Why Sharing the Spotlight is the Secret to Success

Saying no allows you to focus on your priorities, and it empowers others to step up and shine.

- **The "Empowerment through Delegation":** There is someone else who might be a better fit, and delegating empowers their growth.

- **The "Family First Philosophy":** Your priorities, like family needs, take precedence.

- **The "Focus on Your Brilliance":** Your time is best spent where your unique skills can create the most significant impact.

- Example: A local charity asks you to help with their annual bake sale. While it's a worthy cause, your time might be better spent finalizing your manuscript, which can have a broader reach and greater impact.

- Example: Your child's school play coincides with a networking event. Choosing your family shows your true radiance.

- **Example:** A junior colleague expresses interest in learning event planning. You suggest they take the lead on organizing your next book signing, offering guidance along the way.

Beyond the Ego: Sharing the Spotlight

J.K. Rowling

Imagine J.K. Rowling, a single mom on social assistance, hunched over a coffee shop table with a sleeping baby in a stroller beside her. Fueled by caffeine and sheer determination, she scribbles away, the first seeds of the Harry Potter universe taking root. Back then, delegation wasn't an option. Every aspect of her dream, from crafting the story to navigating the publishing world, rested on her shoulders.

Fast forward to a whirlwind of success. The Harry Potter series exploded, captivating readers worldwide. Suddenly, the single mom with a dream was at the helm of a global phenomenon. This is where the power of "beyond the ego" truly shines.

Rowling, fiercely protective of her writing time, knew she couldn't do it all. She built a strong management team, a squad of talented individuals who took on the business aspects – licensing, merchandise, film adaptations – the things that could easily steal her focus. This allowed her to dedicate her energy to her core strength: weaving the magic of Harry Potter's world.

But delegation wasn't just about business. Rowling surrounded herself with talented editors, designers, and other creative collaborators. She understood that a cohesive world requires a symphony of voices. By trusting their expertise, she ensured the series maintained its quality and consistency.

This delegation wasn't just about lightening her load, it was about empowering others to contribute their unique talents to the world she envisioned. The result? A literary phenomenon that continues to enthrall readers of all ages. Rowling's dedication to focus and delegation not only ensured the series' success but also empowered a team to shine alongside her.

Challenges and Considerations:

Letting go can be hard. Imagine the young, fiercely independent Rowling, used to tackling everything herself, now entrusting parts of her dream to others. There were likely moments of doubt and the need to build trust. But Rowling understood that true brilliance often requires a village.

Communication is Key:

Especially in creative endeavors like writing a book series, clear communication is vital. Rowling likely worked closely with her team, ensuring everyone understood the vision for the Harry Potter universe. This open dialogue allowed for collaboration while maintaining the series' core integrity.

J.K. Rowling's journey is an inspiration. It demonstrates that saying no to some tasks isn't about selfishness, it's about focusing on your core strengths and empowering others to contribute theirs. By embracing delegation and focus, you too can create something truly radiant.

*****

Now you are empowered with all the tools you need to navigate life, assertively ask for what you need, and negotiate other options. But what happens when you encounter those people who won't take no for an answer? Chapter 11 The Art Of The "No" Zone Defense: Countering Resistance, Guilt Trips & Manipulation addresses how to apply the tools you've learned and when to walk away.

Chapter 11 The Art Of "No" Zone Defense: Countering Resistance, Guilt & Manipulation

"The most dangerous stories we make up are the narratives that diminish our inherent worthiness. We must reclaim the truth about our lovability, divinity, and creativity."

-Brene Brown

*****

The "Yes, But..." Trap and the Power of Persistence: Leah Says No to Burnout

Leah, fresh out of college, landed her dream job at a prestigious marketing firm. Ambition burned bright in her eyes, and she eagerly devoured every task her demanding boss, Sarah, threw her way. Late nights at the office became a badge of honor, and weekends were sacrificed on the altar of looming deadlines. But the exhaustion gnawed at her like a persistent ache, slowly eclipsing the initial excitement.

One Friday evening, as Sarah piled on yet another "urgent" project requiring a weekend of work, Leah felt a familiar knot of resentment tighten in her stomach. This wasn't sustainable. Taking a deep breath to counter the "people-pleasing autopilot" kicking in, Leah decided to try the "No Zone Defense" techniques she'd been reading about.

"Sarah," Leah started, her voice calm but firm, "I appreciate the trust you've placed in me, but I'm already swamped with deadlines. Taking on this new project wouldn't be feasible without sacrificing the quality of my current work."

Sarah's brow furrowed. "Leah, this is a crucial presentation for a major client. We can't afford any slip-ups."

The Resistance Tactic: The Implied Threat. Leah recognized the attempt to manipulate her fear of jeopardizing the company's success.

"I understand the importance of the client," Leah replied, employing the Art of the Broken Record.

"However, spreading myself too thin will ultimately lead to mistakes. Perhaps we can prioritize the existing deadlines and re-evaluate the timeline for this new project on Monday?"

Sarah sighed, clearly frustrated. "Look, Leah, everyone puts in extra effort here. We're a team, remember?" The Resistance Tactic: The Guilt Trip.

This time, Leah used the Power of Silence. She looked at Sarah, waiting for her to continue without getting drawn into a justification battle.

After a tense moment, Sarah softened slightly. "Alright," she conceded. "Let's connect again on Monday and see how things stand. But in the meantime, can you at least look at the project brief over the weekend?"

Leah, relieved to have navigated the situation, smiled. "Great! Let's work together to figure out the best approach." Finding a Solution Together. While not a complete victory, Leahhad established a boundary and avoided feeling pressured into an unsustainable workload.

This small win was a turning point for Leah. By learning to identify and counter the resistance tactics, she gradually established clear boundaries with Sarah. Weekends became sacrosanct, and late nights were a rarity. Leah discovered that a healthy work-life balance didn't diminish her dedication, but rather fueled her creativity and productivity. She had become a "radiant, resilient champion" of her own time and well-being, all thanks to the power of learning to say "no."

*****

Understanding the Why Behind the Pushback

- **Fear of Disappointment:** People may resist your "no" response because they genuinely rely on you or fear letting you down. This is often the case with family or close friends.

Debbie and the Bake Sale Battle: A "No" Zone Victory

The aroma of freshly baked cookies filled the air as Debbie surveyed the bustling PTA bake sale sign-up sheet. Every year, it felt like a replay of the same stressful scenario. Jay, her well-meaning but overzealous husband, had enthusiastically signed them up to bake twelve dozen cupcakes – again. Memories of last year's marathon baking session, fuelled by gallons of coffee and a desperate need for sleep, flooded back. This year, Debbie was determined to say "no" and reclaim her sanity (and sleep schedule).

Visions of disappointed children and PTA moms giving her the side-eye played in her mind.

Taking a deep breath, Debbie remembered the tools from her "No" Zone defense training. She called Jay, steeling her nerves for the potential resistance. Jay, ever the optimist, launched into a spiel about how much fun it would be to bake together and relive their "college baking days."

Instead of getting sucked into justifications or reminiscing, Debbie used the broken record technique. "Jay, I appreciate you thinking of us, but I don't have the capacity to take on the bake sale this year. I'm swamped with deadlines for my writing project."

Jay, sensing her resolve, tried a new tactic. "Yes, I know you're busy, but what if we just buy some cupcakes from that new bakery downtown? They're supposed to be amazing!"

"I know you're trying to find a solution," Debbie said gently, "but I need to set a strong boundary on my workload right now. However, wouldn't it be fun to volunteer for a different PTA event together? Maybe we could help out with the game booths?"

A surprised silence greeted Debbie's suggestion. Jay paused, considering her words.

"You know what," Jay finally said with a grin, "helping out at the game booths sounds like a blast! We can even wear those silly mascot costumes we always talk about."

*****

Healthy Disagreement vs. Manipulation

It's important to distinguish between healthy disagreement and manipulative tactics. Here's the key difference:

- **Healthy Disagreement:** A respectful exchange of ideas where both parties listen and consider different perspectives. It might lead to a compromise or a simple "agree to disagree."

- **Empathy is Key:** Acknowledge their feelings, even if you disagree with their request. Let them know you understand why they might be disappointed.

Respectful "No"s for a Global World: Building Bridges When Cultures Collide

In the previous section, we explored the power of "no" and the importance of setting boundaries. However, the simple response of saying "no" can take on different meanings when navigating a world of diverse cultures. This section delves into situations where cultural norms might influence how your "no" is perceived, offering strategies to navigate these complexities effectively.

Understanding the Why: Cultural Nuances and "No"

Cultural values play a significant role in shaping expectations around obligations and personal needs. In some collectivist cultures, prioritizing the group needs takes precedence over individual desires. For example, family and community gatherings might be considered paramount, and declining an invitation could be considered disrespectful.

Here's where cultural awareness becomes crucial:

- **Recognize the Difference:** Being aware of your own cultural background and the background of the person you're saying "no" to can help you anticipate potential resistance. Reflect on how your culture views "no" and how it might differ from theirs.

● **Respectful Communication:** When declining a request, frame your response with respect for their cultural values. Acknowledge the importance of their invitation or request, even if you need to decline.

Educate, Don't Justify: Building Understanding Through Explanation

Instead of simply apologizing or making excuses for your "no," focus on explaining your needs and priorities within the context of your own culture. Here's the key difference:

● **Justification:** Often involves apologies or excuses that can come across as dismissive of their cultural perspective. (Example: "I'm so sorry, but I'm just too busy...")

● **Education:** This involves calmly explaining your limitations and needs within your cultural framework. (Example: "In my culture, it's important for me to dedicate time to [your priority], so unfortunately, I won't be able to attend...")

A Balancing Act- Maria and the Family Gathering

Maria, a young American professional, recently married into a large Latinx family. Family gatherings are a cherished tradition, often involving extended family traveling long distances. This year, the gathering falls right in the middle of a crucial work presentation for Maria. Saying "no" feels disrespectful, but attending could jeopardize her career.

Navigating the Situation:

Maria decides to have an open conversation with her spouse, explaining the importance of the presentation in her professional culture. She explores alternative solutions, like attending virtually or participating in a smaller pre-gathering.

By understanding her in-laws' cultural perspective and respectfully explaining her own needs, Maria can navigate this situation with grace and maintain strong family relationships.

Cultural sensitivity is key to navigating resistance to your "no." By educating and respecting cultural differences, you can find solutions that honor both your needs and the values of those around you. Building bridges of understanding through respectful communication paves the way for stronger relationships and a more inclusive global community.

Beyond the Guilt Trip: Setting Boundaries with Pushy People

We've discussed cultural differences and the importance of understanding the "why" behind resistance to your "no." However, sometimes the reason is more straightforward: the person simply wants what they want and might pressure you into a "yes." Here are some examples of how this can play out:

- **The Friend with the Never-Ending Favor List:** A friend constantly bombards you with requests, from last-minute house-sitting to borrowing money. You start to feel drained and taken advantage of.

- **The Persistent Colleague:** A coworker keeps pushing you to take on additional tasks, even though your workload is already heavy. They might use guilt trips or flattery to get you to agree.

- **The Family Outing:** A family member insists on a specific activity for a get-together, even though you know you won't enjoy it. They might try emotional appeals or make you feel like the odd one out for disagreeing.

- **Emotional Appeals:** "It's a family tradition! Don't you want to spend quality time with us?"

- **Guilt Trips:** "Oh, come on, it won't be that bad. Are you really going to disappoint everyone?"

- **Social Pressure:** "Everyone else is excited! Don't you want to be part of the fun?

These situations require a firm but respectful approach to your "no."
Navigating Pushy Requests:

1. **The Broken Record Technique:** Repeat your "no" calmly and confidently, without getting drawn into justifications.

2. **Set Clear Boundaries:** Be upfront about your limitations and politely explain why you can't say yes.
3. **Offer Alternatives:** If possible, alternative solutions that might meet their needs partially without compromising yours. Suggest getting together for part of the event or joining them for a different activity later.

Remember: a healthy "no" is not a rejection; it's setting boundaries to protect your well-being. Your happiness matters too. By communicating effectively and setting boundaries, you can still enjoy family time without enduring activities you despise. You are not obligated to give in to pressure from family, friends or co-workers to do things you don't want to do.

A clear and firm "no" protects your time and well-being. A helpful consideration here would be questioning why you feel guilty? You are not doing anything wrong by saying no so what is driving the emotion and behaviour? Are you trying to avoid conflict by keeping the peace? Which of the 6 Limiting Beliefs does this come from? When you re-frame the original belief you empower yourself to take back your authority and give yourself permission to say no.

Decoding the Guilt Trip: Red Flags of Emotional Manipulation

Recognize The Four Faces of Resistance: We'll different ways people might resist your "no," from passive-aggressive sighs to full-blown anger. Understanding these tactics empowers you to respond calmly and effectively.

Face #1: The Silent Sigh
This is the disapproval tactic or "I'm not happy with your decision."

- **Scenario:** You decline an invitation to a weekend getaway with friends, citing your need to catch up on work. A friend lets out a dramatic sigh, followed by a long silence.

- **Defense Strategy:** Acknowledge the sigh with a simple, "Okay," and politely explain your desire to stay in this time. You can suggest an alternative, like a quick coffee catch-up during the week.

Face #2: The Manipulation Gambler:
A tactic used to control your decision-making involving bullying, guilt trips or emotional blackmail, to pressure you into a "yes."

- **Scenario:** Your adult child calls, asking you to last-minute housesit for their vacation, despite knowing you have important errands planned. They manipulate you by saying, "But Mom, you're the only one we can trust! We'd be so stressed if we couldn't go."

- **Defense Strategy:** Recognize the guilt for what it is and remind yourself of your pre-existing commitments. You can say, "I understand you want a relaxing vacation, but I already have plans I can't reschedule. Perhaps you can find a pet sitter or house-swapping option?"

Face #3: The Anger Antagonizer:
A tactic used to control with fear or instigate a fawning response to avoid a confrontation so you give in with a yes to stop further escalation from them.

- **Scenario:** You decline a request from a colleague to take on their workload while they're on vacation. They become defensive and accuse you of not being a team player.

- **Defense Strategy:** Stay calm and don't get drawn into an argument. You can say, "I appreciate you needing help, but I have a full plate right now. Perhaps we can talk to our manager about finding a solution that works for everyone." If the situation escalates, you can excuse yourself from the conversation.

Face #4: The "Just This Once" Joker

A tactic used to down play the amount of time or energy the request will actually involve or the frequency that favors will be expected in the future.

- **Scenario:** Your neighbor asks you to watch their dog for the entire weekend, framing it as a small favor. They downplay the inconvenience, saying, "It'll be no trouble at all, just walk him twice a day. We'd really appreciate it!"

- **Defense Strategy:** Be wary of requests disguised as "just this once" or "no big deal." If it doesn't fit your schedule or lifestyle, politely decline. You can offer an alternative solution, like recommending a dog walker or suggesting they shorten their trip.

Reclaim Your Power: The Art of Saying "No" Without Apology: Breaking Free from the Guilt Trap

Recognizing a guilt trip is a crucial first step, but how do you break free from its manipulative grip? This section delves into strategies for "detoxifying" the situation and reclaiming your power to say "no" with confidence.

Identifying the Red Flags of Manipulation:

Guilt trips rarely arrive with flashing neon signs. They often come disguised as caring or concerned statements.

Spotting the Guilt Grenades: Watch out for phrases that trigger feelings of obligation or shame:

- **The "Yes, But..." Trap:** This seemingly agreeable phrase creates a false sense of compromise, but the "but" is often followed by unreasonable demands. (Example: "Yes, I can help you move, but only if I get to pick the takeout place afterward.")

- **The Accusatory Opener:** Phrases like "You never..." or "You always..." launch an attack on your character, making you feel defensive and shifting the focus away from the situation. (Example: "You never help out around here! Don't you care about me?")

- **The Emotional Appeal:** Statements dripping with sentiment like "If you really cared about me..." or "This will really hurt me" attempt to leverage your emotions to manipulate your decision. (Example: "If you were a true friend, you'd cancel your plans and come to my event.")

- **Playing the Victim:** Guilt trippers often position themselves as the victim, implying your "no" causes them undue hardship, guilt, or sadness. (Example: "I worked so hard on this party, and now you're not coming? It really hurts my feelings.")

- **Identify the Manipulation:** Acknowledge the guilt for what it is- a tactic used to control you through emotional pressure. Don't get sucked into the guilt spiral; instead, see it for what it is- a manipulative attempt to get their way.

- **Shift the Focus:** Instead of dwelling on their disappointment (real or perceived), turn your attention to your own needs and values. Ask yourself powerful questions like, "Does this request align with my desired end result?" or "Does saying yes compromise my well-being?" Focusing on your core values helps maintain a clear perspective.

- **Respond with Clarity:** Now that you've re-framed the situation, it's time to communicate your "no" with clarity and without apology. You can say, "I understand you were looking for this, but I can't take on this request right now. I have a lot on my plate, and saying yes would be too much to manage effectively."

- **Reframe the Situation: You're in Control-** Once you identify these red flags, it's time to re-frame the situation. Here are some steps to take back control: Your "no" is a complete sentence. You don't owe justifications or elaborate explanations. A clear and concise response delivered with confidence demonstrates your emotional resilience and protects your boundaries. These steps, you can break free from the guilt trap, dismantle the manipulation, and confidently say "no" while maintaining healthy relationships.

The strategies do not change when dealing with people who do not want to accept your initial no. The tactics they use in their negotiations (or lack of) are the real information you need to be aware of because that will be your emotional triggers that may cause the fawn reaction in the fight or flight response. The more self-awareness you have that this is going on, the sooner you can recognize the strategy you need to apply. The more you do it the more familiar and comfortable it will become.

CONCLUSION

"I am a free spirit. Some people don't like that, but that's who I am."-
Princess Dianna

*****

You Are the Architect of Your Radiance

Congratulations! You've reached the conclusion of "Radiant Resilience." Throughout this journey, we've explored the art of saying "no" – not as a rejection, but as a powerful communication tool for empowerment to be your own creative warrior.

Trust: The Bedrock of Radiant Resilience

Trust, a cornerstone of healthy relationships and a vital core value is woven throughout the fabric of "Radiant Resilience." Consider it the fertile ground where your sense of security and ability to thrive and truly blossom. Most importantly, always trust yourself.

Now, it's time to take these strategies and weave them into the vibrant tapestry of your life, designing a future where you shine your brightest. Here are some key takeaways to illuminate your path:

- **Desired End Results: Chart Your Course:** Before responding to any request, envision your ideal future. What does a life of radiance look like for you? Are your actions propelling you towards those goals, or pulling you off course? Make "no" your compass, guiding you toward a life that aligns with your deepest desires.

- **Core Values: Your Guiding Light:** Live by your core values. These are the fundamental principles that guide your decisions. When faced with a request, ask yourself: does this align with my values? Saying "no" to things that contradict your values protects your integrity and empowers you to live authentically.

- **Self-Care: Fuel Your Radiance And Confidence:** We can't pour from an empty cup. Prioritizing self-care practices nourishes your mind, body, and spirit, transforming your confidence. When you feel rested, recharged, and connected to yourself, you naturally project a sense of calm strength.

- **Rejuvenating Practices:** Whether it's a long bath, a mindful walk in nature, or spending time with loved ones, incorporate activities that bring you joy and renewal.

- **Nurturing Your Body:** Prioritize healthy eating, adequate sleep, and regular exercise. When you take care of your physical well-being, you'll have more energy and stamina to tackle your day with confidence.

- **Quieting the Inner Critic:** Self-care also includes cultivating self-compassion. Practice affirmations and positive self-talk to counter negative thoughts that can erode your confidence.

- **Journaling for Self-Discovery:** Journaling is a powerful tool for self-reflection. Use it to explore your core values, identify areas for improvement, and track your progress. Regular journaling fosters self-awareness, a crucial ingredient for making confident and empowered decisions.

- **Gratitude Meditations: Cultivating Abundance:** Gratitude is a radiance booster. Regularly cultivate an attitude of gratitude through meditation or simply reflecting on the things you're thankful for. Gratitude grounds you and empowers you to say "no" to things that don't serve your highest good.

- **Mastering Your Time:** Time is your most precious resource. Become a master of time management techniques to prioritize tasks and optimize your schedule. By saying "no" to time wasters, you free up space for the activities that ignite your radiance.

- **Assertive Communication Skills: Speaking Your Truth:** Effective communication is essential for saying "no" with grace. Hone your assertive communication skills to express your declines clearly, confidently, and with respect.

- **Delegation: Empowering Others to Shine:** Delegation isn't about dodging responsibility; it's about leveraging the strengths of others. Don't be afraid to delegate tasks that drain your energy or fall outside your core expertise. By empowering others, you free up your time and energy to focus on what truly matters.

The Power of "No" - It's Not Just for You

Throughout this book, we've focused on the transforming power of you saying "no." But the concept goes beyond your responses. Just as you have the right to set boundaries and prioritize your needs, so do others.

What does it mean when someone says no to you? It is not a personal rejection. It's an opportunity to practice empathy and understanding. Perhaps their schedule is already overloaded, or the request doesn't align with their values. No matter their reason, you now have the skills to keep an open mind and look for other opportunities.

Shifting Your Perspective

- **Focus on Understanding:** Instead of feeling slighted or frustrated, try to see things from their perspective. Ask clarifying questions to understand their reasoning.

- **Respect Their Boundaries:** Just as you deserve to have your "no" respected, so do they. Accept their decision gracefully and move on.

- **Open Communication:** If a "no" feels unexpected, open communication can be helpful. Express your understanding and see if there's a way to adjust the request to accommodate everyone's needs.

The Power of Empathy

By approaching "no" from others with empathy, you strengthen your relationships and foster a more collaborative environment. It demonstrates respect for their time and priorities, creating a sense of trust and mutual give and receive.

Remember, "no" is a powerful tool for everyone. When used with grace and empathy, it paves the way for open communication resulting in stronger, healthier relationships and more fulfillment and satisfaction for everyone.

So, embrace the power of "no," prioritize self-care, cultivate confidence, and thrive on your journey to a life filled with purpose, passion, and radiant success. You are the architect of your own radiance. Go forth and design a life that allows your brilliance to shine!

Remember, "no" is not an ending, but a powerful beginning. It's a tool that allows you to focus on what truly matters, paving the way for your radiance to shine brighter than ever before.

The Empowered Woman's Manifesto

*****

Carry this manifesto as a shield and a sword. It will empower you to navigate life's inevitable challenges with unwavering confidence. Remember, setbacks are not failures, they're stepping stones. When doubt creeps in, revisit the tools you've acquired. Practice your "no" phrases, silence the inner critic, and realign with your vision.

This journey doesn't end here. This is just the beginning. Go forth, and illuminate the world with your strength, your resilience, and your unwavering confidence.

About the author

Joanne C. Pugh is a Canadian author who lives in Ontario, Canada. She is a mother of two boys, Correy and Brandon. She attended College in 2010 in the Addiction and Community Services Program earning her diploma after fulfilling her student placement plus an additional 160 hours of volunteer time with the Toronto Bail Program in the Criminal Justice Department. Joanne went on to work with male and female homeless youth ages 16-27 and was a Facilitator of the Anger Management Program through Operation Springboard.

Her hobbies include outdoor adventures, solo wilderness camping, hiking, waterfalls, whitewater rafting and pyrography. She loves to travel, has visited Egypt and plans to go to Africa for a wilderness retreat. Joanne has dedicated herself to learning several healing modalities including Reiki, Crystals, E.F.T., Ho'oponopono, N.L.P. and volunteered thousands of hours working with members in the community through the healing power of music and art with Love Project Women And Art and Hopefest Music For Miracles in collaboration with SickKids Hospital, organizing and promoting fundraising events to raise money for Marnie's Studio. Joanne was a member of Toastmaster's International and mentored the youth public speaking group ages 12-18 and participated in a Polar Plunge in 2023 to raise funds for the Ontario Special Olympics.

Joanne's greatest passion is creating with others to achieve success and overcome personal challenges. She has a "we" and "us" attitude and believes no one succeeds alone.

www.ingramcontent.com/pod-product-compliance
Lightning Source LLC
Chambersburg PA
CBHW030837090426
42737CB00009B/1002